CRISIS COUNSELING

Creative Pastoral Care and Counseling Series

Howard W. Stone, Editor

BOOKS IN THE SERIES

CREATIVE PASTORAL CARE AND COUNSELING SERIES

CRISIS COUNSELING

Third Edition

Howard W. Stone

FORTRESS PRESS   MINNEAPOLIS

For Karen

CRISIS COUNSELING
Third Edition

Copyright © 2009 Fortress Press, an imprint of Augsburg Fortress. All rights reserved. Except for brief quotations in critical articles or reviews, no part of this book may be reproduced in any manner without prior written permission from the publisher. Visit http://www.augsburgfortress.org/copyrights/contact.asp or write to Permissions, Augsburg Fortress, Box 1209, Minneapolis, MN 55440.

First edition published in 1976 by Fortress Press; revised edition 1993.

Scripture quotations unless otherwise noted are from the New Revised Standard Version Bible, copyright © 1989 by the Division of Christian Education of the National Council of the Churches of Christ in the United States. All rights reserved.

Scripture marked TEV is taken from the Good News Translation—Second Edition, copyright © 1992 by American Bible Society. Used by permission.

Cover design: Michelle L. N. Cook
Cover art: photo © Russell Thurston/Getty Images

Library of Congress Cataloging-in-Publication Data
Stone, Howard W.
  Crisis counseling / Howard W. Stone. — 3rd ed.
    p. cm. — (Creative pastoral care and counseling series)
  Includes bibliographical references.
  ISBN 978-0-8006-6352-0 (alk. paper)
  1. Pastoral counseling. 2. Crisis intervention (Mental health services) I. Title.
  BV4012.2.S75 2009
  253.5—dc22
                    2008036610

The paper used in this publication meets the minimum requirements of American National Standard for Information Sciences—Permanence of Paper for Printed Library Materials, ANSI Z329.48-1984.

Manufactured in the U.S.A.

CONTENTS

PREFACE

9/11. Before September 11, 2001, those three digits were just numbers. They'd have no significance for you unless they represented a birthday, a locker, a PIN, the number to call in an emergency. Now, they represent not only an earth-shattering event but also the way that event left us, in a world that we fear will never be the same.

I talked with one of the ministers who responded to the devastation at the World Trade Center; she told me that whenever she walked along the line of people waiting to find information on missing loved ones and they saw her clerical collar, they would grab her, hug her, sob, and tell stories about the person who was missing. There was no introduction, rarely an exchange of names. These people just needed someone who cared, to know that there was a God who was for them and with them in the twisted metal and strewn rubble, in the chaos, in their fear and bewilderment and loss.

When walls are falling around us and much of what we have known and held safe is crumbling, the pastoral care of Christians (clergy and lay alike) is a vital lifeline to comfort, restoration, and hope. It does not erase tragedy; the loss always remains. But pastoral care can steady us as we walk through the valley of the shadow of death, as we begin to pick up the pieces and try to make sense of what has happened. It helps that someone is with us as the representative presence of the church. God, in the person of the pastoral caregiver, is walking the lines of troubled people and offering comfort, a listening ear, an assurance that beyond this dark valley lies the possibility of light, warmth, meaning, and purpose.

It is a continuing surprise for me that *Crisis Counseling* has been so well received—and for so many years. *Crisis Counseling* now has been translated into five languages and has met a response, not only in the United States but also in countries around the world, that surprises and gratifies me. I have walked into pastor's studies in England, Ireland, Japan, South Africa, and Venezuela, as well as the United States, and seen a copy of this book on the shelf.

I believe that the response to *Crisis Counseling* results from a need—and a concern—that clergy and other pastoral caregivers feel with regard to the crisis situations they encounter. In most communities, the pastor is often the first recourse for people whose walls are crumbling. When someone in a crisis arrives at your door, you are on the spot—needed, and now. This certainly was the experience of my friend who walked the lines of waiting family members after 9/11. People in crisis rely on you to know what to do, to steer them through emergency, tragedy, disaster, and loss. Often they feel paralyzed; it is up to you to help them get moving again.

Crises can be frightening experiences. *Crisis Counseling* exists because of my own concerns when responding to crisis situations. Before I attended graduate school, before I even had the idea of writing a book, I began collecting questions and reflections from people in crisis whom I encountered in my ministry: what helped, what did not, how people acted, what I could read that would better prepare me for the next crisis.

Now, many years after the first publication of *Crisis Counseling* and a revised edition, it is time for a third edition. I have changed. Recent research has altered some ideas about crises. Students, colleagues, and counselees have asked questions, made suggestions, shared insights, and shaped my thinking. Above all, the world has changed. New or newly named diseases and conditions—such as Alzheimer's, PTSD, and AIDS—are either coming to light or spreading. People are living on the edge. No one feels entirely safe. Modern existence seems to be a crisis waiting to happen. Still, though the world may have changed forever, our basic human needs remain the same.

What began as an updating of *Crisis Counseling*, therefore, gradually became a more extensive revision than I had planned. I changed and added more material on suicide, intervention in volatile or hazardous situations, and personal safety of the minister. (Several of my acquaintances have been injured while intervening in a crisis, and one helper in my area was killed.) Safety for both the person in need and the pastoral caregiver is now even more critical. Helper burnout is also an issue.

The second and third editions of *Crisis Counseling* reflect culture shifts as well as changes in the field. Although crisis intervention theory arose primarily from psychotherapeutic theory and practice involving the individual, this revision places greater emphasis on caring for groups of individuals, especially marriage and family systems. After all, in the history of pastoral care in the church, pastoral care has always been offered to couples, families, and whole communities.

In the time that intervened since the second edition, I worked with two psychology professors and one communications professor at my university to test further the ideas related in this book. We asked all of the individuals in a large Protestant church who experienced a crisis during a specific period of time to describe what was most and least helpful as they faced the crisis. Chapter 6 of this third edition describes what we learned from the study (Stone et al. 2003; Stone et al. 2004).

Crisis Counseling unites the historic skills of pastoral care and counseling with current methods of crisis intervention from the fields of psychology and psychotherapy. Like the original edition, the present book is written for ministers—both clergy and lay—who are called upon to care for those in crisis; like the previous editions, its concepts and methods will be of value to mental health professionals and crisis hotline volunteers as well. *Crisis Counseling* discusses the minister's role as a crisis intervener. It incorporates my understanding of recent crisis intervention theory. I urge the reader to give particular attention to chapter 2, because a thorough grasp of the dynamics of crisis is vital for effective crisis management.

Chapter 3 is the core of the book; it presents a detailed methodology of crisis intervention. Chapter 4 suggests how we as pastoral caregivers can handle the especially difficult crises and how we can protect ourselves and those who are experiencing a crisis. Chapter 5 illustrates these methods of caregiving with case studies that demonstrate the wide variety of situations that benefit from crisis intervention methods. I have updated several of the cases and added an additional case. (All cases presented in this book, though modified to ensure confidentiality, are taken from my own pastoral care and counseling ministry and that of other ministers.) Finally, chapter 6 addresses the whole community of faith and its role in offering care and support to people in their times of greatest need. Here I relate the findings of the aforementioned study of church members who suffered crises and the help they received.

Some terms may require clarification. Although this book is titled *Crisis Counseling*, it might better fall under the heading of pastoral care; many of the crisis situations described need far more than a standard fifty-minute hour in the pastor's office. I use the terms *crisis counseling* and *crisis intervention* interchangeably to include both pastoral counseling and pastoral care (a home visit, a typical counseling session, a telephone conversation, or even arranging for other people to do the helping); a better term might be *pastoral conversation*. To identify the people involved, I make the following distinctions: *clergy* and *pastor* refer to ordained ministers, priests, and rabbis. *Minister, pastoral carer, helper,* and *caregiver* refer to laypersons as well as the ordained. The person in crisis is identified in a variety of ways, such as troubled person, person in distress, counselee, and parishioner.

In this brief space I cannot adequately express appreciation to the many people who helped and influenced me in the development of *Crisis Counseling*. Nevertheless, I would like to give my special thanks to John Landgraf, Alton Goodenberger, Herbert Anderson, Howard Clinebell, Brian Feille, and David Lott for reading present or previous versions of the manuscript and offering valuable suggestions. I am grateful to over thirty-five years of students for their enthusiasm, questions, and contributions to my thinking. I also want to thank the military chaplains for helping to develop the ideas in chapter 4. To the readers of the first two editions of *Crisis Counseling* who helped to shape this new manuscript by sending comments, criticism, and ideas—thank you, and keep writing; I value your feedback. Finally, to Karen Stone, who helped prepare all three versions of the manuscript, I can never fully express my gratitude . . . but I will surely try.

1

THE MINISTER
AS CRISIS COUNSELOR

I was working in my study early one Wednesday evening when I received a telephone call from Sandra Chase, a woman in the Philadelphia congregation where I was serving as assistant pastor.*

Sandra was panic stricken. She said she had to see me right away because her seventeen-year-old son, Gary, had just informed her that he was going to elope that weekend. She was passionately opposed to the youthful marriage, but Gary was equally adamant. They wanted help.

Before I had a chance to ask whether Sandra had called the senior pastor, she reminded me that he was out of town. I agreed to meet with Sandra, her husband Leonard, Gary, and his fiancée Jeanne, later that evening.

This was my first crisis in the role of pastor. As I drove to the Chases' home, I felt fear: I knew other people were counting on me because I was a minister, but I did not have much of an idea about what to do.

Both teenagers seemed mature and were willing to talk. I had also called Jeanne's parents, but they would not even speak with me. (A visit to their home a few days later brought the same result.) Sandra and Leonard finally decided to support the couple when they realized the wedding was going to take place with or without their approval. But they wanted a church wedding for their son. It was relatively easy to help the four reach a compromise on that point. After Gary and Jeanne returned from their elopement, the church's rite for the Blessing of a Civil Marriage, much like a wedding, was conducted with congregation, family, and friends sharing in the event.

The young couple came to me for several counseling sessions afterward, each time discussing where they would live, finances, sex, children, and how they would deal with relatives (especially her parents). Some bad feelings remained; the elder Chases were

---

* All names have been changed and, as necessary, situations modified to protect the privacy of the individuals described.

particularly resentful toward Jeanne's parents for "abandoning" the couple. But the church ceremony, and the willingness of most of the people involved to get together and talk, helped Jeanne and Gary start on a good foot at a time of life that can often be exceedingly hazardous. Although not a catastrophe on the level of 9/11 or Hurricane Katrina, the successful resolution of this crisis may have helped them deal with future crises.

All of us experience crises from time to time. We reach an edge, an emergency, a moment arrives when a decision must be made, a problem solved, a significant issue dispatched, a terrifying or agonizing situation confronted. We are constrained to make elemental choices. Crises force us to recognize that we are unprotected and naked before others, God, and even ourselves. Indeed, Charles Gerkin (1987, 32–33) describes a crisis as an extreme or boundary condition in which

> the fundamental contradiction between human aspirations and finite possibilities becomes visible in such a way as to demand attention. In the situational crisis we are confronted with our human vulnerability, our finitude, the utter impossibility of our deepest hopes and wishes. In that situation a most elemental choice is forced upon persons that is at its core a religious or "faith" choice. Either they must defend themselves against the contradiction with whatever human defense is possible, be that denial or heroic courage, or they must open themselves to the vulnerability of the unknown future, trusting in the power and care of God coming out of the change and contingency of the unknown.

In one way or another, whether ministers like it or not, they are faced with crises in people's lives. Crisis ministry has been part of pastoral care throughout many centuries; indeed, Christians have learned to expect their pastors to be with them at such times (Stone et al. 2003; Stone et al. 2004).

A literature and methodology referred to as "crisis intervention" emerged in the second half of the last century in the fields of psychology, psychiatry, and social work. The purpose of this book is to blend recent developments in crisis intervention from these mental health fields with the skills of pastoral caregiving. I will not survey various methods of crisis intervention practice, but, rather, share a particular method of intervention based upon theories of crisis—a method that has a broad theoretical base and has been effective in practice.

KEY CONCEPTS

A crisis can be understood as a crucial time and a turning point. In the present context it is the term for an individual's internal reaction to an external hazard. It involves a temporary loss of coping abilities, a paralysis of action. Any definition of crisis makes a tacit assumption that the emotional dysfunction is reversible. Persons in crisis are not necessarily mentally ill; they are simply responding to a hazardous circumstance. If they effectively cope with the threat, a return to former levels of functioning will result.

Although this definition speaks of crisis as an internal reaction of an individual, one must not forget that crises also happen to families (Pittman 1987). When a crisis precipitated by some threatening external event comes to bear on a system (e.g., a family), it weakens the internal boundaries of the system, and that system is more open, more receptive to help from the outside. Crises strike not only isolated individuals but also families, extended families, congregations, and systems great and small. Just think about the impact that the death of John F. Kennedy or the events of 9/11 had upon an entire nation. In 2005 Hurricane Katrina had a profound, life-changing (and perhaps culture-changing) impact on the people of New Orleans and the Gulf Coast communities, and even the nation.

Two basic types of crisis exist: *developmental* and *situational.* Normal developmental crises are the predictable, though critical, experiences that everyone goes through in the maturation process, such as the turmoil attendant upon adolescence or middle age. Situational crises are exceptional and unpredictable; they are the upheavals resulting from unusual circumstances or events such as divorce or a disabling accident.

Situational crises might arise in connection with the loss of a job, of a support person, or of a position of status and respect; an incapacitating accident, illness, or operation; the death of a friend, child, or spouse; one's own impending death; the discovery of marital infidelity; retirement; an unwanted pregnancy; moving to a new city; learning that one is HIV positive; a national disaster or massive calamity such as war, hurricane, or terrorist attack; inheriting children from a previous marriage; abortion; arrest or incarceration; sudden religious conversion; miscarriage; premature birth; post-traumatic stress disorder (PTSD); birth of a less-than-perfect child; rape or incest; loss of welfare money; entering a retirement home; parents coming to live with their married children—the list could go on and on. Any event that threatens significant change or loss to a person or a family may precipitate a situational crisis.

The aim of pastoral crisis intervention—and the aim of this book—is to help individuals and families deal with situational crises. Crisis intervention refers to a method of aiding individuals and family systems to cope with these emotionally decisive moments in their lives. It includes pastoral counseling as well as other forms of pastoral caregiving, and involves clergy as well as laypersons. It includes all helping activities designed to influence the course of a particular crisis so that those caught in its turmoil can return to their previous level of functioning and possibly even achieve an enhanced ability to contend with future crises.

Ministers entering into an individual or family crisis have the dual objective of reducing the impact of the crisis precipitating event and using the critical situation to help those affected strengthen their skills for solving future problems by learning more effective ways of coping. A crisis calls for new action, and its challenge has the potential to stimulate new ways of responding, increase capacity for living, and enhance mental and spiritual maturity. Crises can be the impetus for personal theological reflection because crisis situations raise elemental issues about life and faith (Stone 1996; Stone and Duke 2006). Crisis intervention is not just Band-Aid therapy; it is also growth oriented.

UNIQUE POSITION AND PERSPECTIVE

Clergy find themselves in a unique position for crisis intervention. For example, grief automatically brings the bereaved into the minister's compass. Pastors are often among the first to be sought out when crises arise, and are natural crisis interveners for a number of reasons.

First, clergy have a core of previously established relationships with people in the congregation. More than anyone else in the community, with the possible exception of the family doctor, they have cared for families during normal developmental crises and periods of stress. A pastor may have guided a family through some previous situational crisis and therefore have specific knowledge not only of how the family handles stress but also intervention methods that were effective for them in the past.

Second, pastors have the advantage of immediacy; due to the clergy's availability and pastoral initiative, persons coming for help will not face weeks or even months of waiting lists, medical scrutiny, or the taking of long case histories. Unlike many other professionals, pastors can go where the people are. They are mobile, not tied to an office or bureaucratic red tape. They have always been able to make visits or schedule counseling appointments in places other than the office—traditionally in the home of the troubled persons. Visitation in hospital, workplace, and home helps pastors achieve a greater breadth of relationship. They come to know people in many more ways than the average psychiatrist or psychologist can know them; for example, caregivers in the church who observe that a family in serious crisis is not seeking help can seize the initiative, make pastoral visits, and offer assistance.

Third, clergy enjoy access to systems. Persons in crisis often are helped by the involvement of as many significant other people as possible. Unlike many mental health professionals who have a strong individualistic focus, the clergy are oriented toward dealing with families, friends, and relatives, and can call on them for assistance during the crisis.

Ministers offering crisis caregiving also are unique in their ability to draw upon a support group from within the congregation. Therapists have no such source of committed individuals upon whom they can rely. Church members who volunteer to call or visit persons in distress offer not only assistance but also a sense of belonging that can offset loneliness and isolation.

The community of faith is not only a specific geographical area, or a particular congregation of believers, but a common level of humanity that brings out the individual capacities of each person. It is not necessarily a place or a purpose, a size or a location, but the experience that one has in encountering others. The community of faith is constantly attuned to the word of God in each individual situation. For example, the word of God for a woman grieving the loss of her husband may mean no more than sitting with her; such a word is not necessarily a verbal exercise. Where such community exists in a local congregation, persons in crisis are offered the support and caring of other members of the household of faith, the representative presence of the church.

Furthermore, to those in crisis, the very authority attributed to the pastor can serve the restoration of perspective and hope so desperately needed. "The person in crisis is one who has begun to lose perspective, feel anxious and helpless, often depressed and worthless, frequently without hope, whose future seems to be blocked out, who even has lost sight of some of his or her own past. Faith . . . is a direct counterforce to the dynamics of crisis" (Switzer 1986, 259).

Howard Clinebell (1984, 184) points out that "in crises and losses people often confront their spiritual hungers, the emptiness of their lives, and the poverty of their values and relationships." In the face of such emptiness, pastors (who are trained to deal with questions of meaning and value) can help people rediscover that living in relationship with a loving and faithful God provides meaning even in the midst of tragedy.

Thus, *perspective* is a major area of difference between pastoral crisis intervention and crisis intervention offered by nonchurch mental health professionals. Ministers and mental health professionals may use many of the same intervention methods, but they approach them from different points of view. I have found that with people in crisis, questions concerning the meaning of suffering, life, death, and pain almost inevitably arise. No matter how troubled people depict their problems—mental, psychiatric, interpersonal, or intrapsychic—all crises are religious at their core, as Gerkin pointed out. They involve ultimate issues with which one must come to terms in the end.

Care and counseling offered by pastors is spiritual in both its final and basic sense. LeRoy Aden (1968, 174) describes "final" in this regard as that which is ultimate from a long-term viewpoint, the end point of a process, whereas "basic" points to whatever is ultimate for humanity "in the present moment, to the depth dimension of a particular moment of time." Aden goes on to say that ministers' final and basic concerns differ from those of psychotherapists. Like all helpers, ministers must grapple with people's immediate problems; but "pastoral counseling has a different guiding image of our plight and rescue, and therefore it often perceives in the client's verbalizations a different struggle and endpoint."

The pastor who witnesses the despair of a person who has suffered abuse and abandonment in childhood, endured years of hardship and failure, and now faces another emotionally hazardous situation, can understand and convey the relevance of such theological concepts as theodicy (the goodness of God in the face of all the evil in the world), sacrifice, sin, grace, faith, and hope (for further discussion of theodicy, see Stone 1996).

Many mental health professionals have recognized the importance of the spiritual dimension to those encountering problems of living. Carl Jung (1949, 264) wrote, "Among all my patients in the second half of life (that is to say, over thirty-five) there has not been one whose problem in the last resort was not that of finding a religious outlook on life." Viktor Frankl (1997, 121), who spent three bleak years in a Nazi prison camp, strongly emphasized the need for meaning in life: "Woe to him who saw no more sense in his life, no aim, no purpose, and therefore no point in carrying on. He was soon lost."

Ministers unquestionably bring to people's crises distinct advantages and perspectives. Chief of these may be a relationship through which people in distress receive the clear sense that life has meaning, purpose, and hope.

2

THE DYNAMICS OF CRISIS

Meanwhile Saul, still breathing threats and murder against the disciples of the Lord, went to the high priest and asked him for letters to the synagogues at Damascus, so that if he found any who belonged to the Way, men or women, he might bring them bound to Jerusalem. Now as he was going along and approaching Damascus, suddenly a light from heaven flashed around him. He fell to the ground and heard a voice saying to him, "Saul, Saul, why do you persecute me?" He asked, "Who are you, Lord?" The reply came, "I am Jesus, whom you are persecuting. But get up and enter the city, and you will be told what you are to do." The men who were traveling with him stood speechless because they heard the voice but saw no one. Saul got up from the ground, and though his eyes were open, he could see nothing; so they led him by the hand and brought him into Damascus. For three days he was without sight, and neither ate nor drank.

—Acts 9:1-9

This passage from the New Testament is one of the most notable accounts of a sudden religious conversion, one event that can precipitate a crisis. Saul's experience was more remarkable than many conversions, resulting as it did from a sudden, blinding vision. But in spite of—or even because of—these extreme circumstances, the story illustrates how such an experience can bring about a crisis in one's life.

Saul's dramatic conversion, occurring as he walked along the sunbaked Roman road outside Damascus, affected him physically: when he opened his eyes "he could see nothing" and had to be led by the hand into the city. The event affected him mentally: he questioned his old beliefs and actions. Paul was changed spiritually as well: one of the most vigorous persecutors of Christianity, he became not only an ardent promoter of the faith but a brilliant theologian who wrote of the life of faith in clear and moving prose. Finally, the conversion affected him emotionally, so much so that he abstained from food and drink for several days. Paul's conversion caused a crisis, it being a turning point that affected every aspect of his life. He would never be the same—nor would the church.

A sound theoretical understanding is basic for effective ministry in a crisis. The purpose of this chapter is to describe the theory of crisis: how a crisis develops and what characteristics mark its occurrence. Most people realize that crucial moments, such as that in Paul's life, occur in their own lives, some becoming crises and others not. Because the methodology of crisis caregiving works best for those who are actually in crisis, it is critical for helpers to examine what occurs in a situational crisis.

HOW A CRISIS DEVELOPS

A crisis occurs as an *internal* response to an *external* hazardous event. It is important not to confuse the crisis with the precipitating event. To this end it may be helpful to think of the development of a crisis in terms of four major elements (see diagram 1). The first is the *stimulus* or *precipitating event*. This is the external peril—such as death, divorce, or loss of a job—which theorists describe as an emotionally hazardous event.

Diagram 1

Precipitating event ⟶ Appraisal ⟶ Resources and coping methods ⟶ Crisis

The second element of crisis development is the *appraisal of the situation*. It is what one makes of the precipitating event, one's perception of it as a hazard or a threat. For a crisis to occur, people must view the precipitator as a profound threat to their well-being or to the well-being of their family. They see it as a very dangerous situation, one that most likely will adversely affect their lives.

Everyone has a unique way of looking at a particular event. For example, one appraises the death of a close friend in terms of the past relationship with the deceased and one's previous experiences of loss; the appraisal also varies with the personality of each person affected. The immediacy of the loss, as well as its scope and impact for the bereaved, determines to a great extent whether a crisis will develop. Thus, the widow of a twenty-six-year marriage who was deeply involved in the life of her husband will most likely perceive a greater loss than will the deceased's business acquaintances, whose relationships with him were limited to infrequent contacts. (Such a death could have a significant impact on the employees of the company he managed, however; they could appraise the death as a serious threat to their financial security and possibly go into crisis.)

The third factor leading to the development of a crisis is *coping methods and personal resources*. Coping methods are the manner in which people respond to problems; they are the strategies or steps one takes to resolve difficulties. Each person marshals external resources (such as friends, relatives, clergy, and physician) and internal resources (such as the ability to face and handle new situations, problem-solving and communication skills) to meet the perceived threat. The adequacy of such resources and coping methods affects the extent to which an individual will experience the threat as a crisis.

Richard S. Lazarus (1966, 153) writes that "when the individual discovers some important motive or value is being threatened, coping activity is mobilized by virtue of this threat, by virtue of the cognition that 'My life, health, wealth, or cherished social relationships are in danger.'" The goal of coping is the reduction or elimination of the appraised threat. If coping methods reduce the threat, a crisis is forestalled.

But if one's coping methods do not diminish the threat, a *crisis* will almost certainly occur. The key to the development of a crisis is that the person's appraisal process (perception, how they see it) deems the precipitating event a serious threat, and the person's coping process does not quickly mitigate the threatening situation. Most theorists and practitioners agree that the resulting acute crisis usually lasts a maximum of six weeks, typically less, even though the aftereffects of any crisis may continue for years. The crisis phase of grief, for example, is only a short measure of the full skein of bereavement.

Thus, a crisis is not an external event, although such an event usually is a precipitator. Instead, a crisis is what happens within people and families as a *response* to that event.

When all the employees of a small-town mine in Pennsylvania were laid off indefinitely after a protracted strike, they reacted differently because of their varying perceptions of the layoff and according to the diversity of their coping methods and resources. Michael Pulaski never cared much for his job, preferring his work as a handyman on evenings and weekends. He was saving money for his retirement, which he hoped would be no more than a few years off. When the union struck, Michael circulated cards advertising his home improvement services and called people he had worked for in the past to see if they had other jobs for him or could refer him to others who might need things fixed in their homes. He and his wife did some cutting in their budget. Michael had adequate financial resources, interpersonal relationships, and internal strengths, and he and his wife weathered the layoff with no real experience of a crisis.

Other mine workers, like Allen Daniels, lacked Michael's resources, appraised the event as catastrophic, and went into a severe crisis. Allen experienced the layoff as an affront to his manhood. He became irritable and autocratic at home. He and his wife came to see me not because of the layoff at the mine, but because Mrs. Daniels was "fed up" with the way Allen was acting and she wanted a divorce. It took several counseling sessions to bring about a reasonable resolution of their situation. The two families clearly experienced the same precipitating event in disparate ways. For one it did not cause even a mild crisis, while for the other it shook the foundations of a twenty-year marriage.

CHARACTERISTICS OF CRISES

A useful way to understand what takes place in any given crisis is to consider the marks of a crisis. Crisis-intervention theory asserts that although the precipitators of crises vary greatly (death, infidelity, accident), all share particular patterns. This generic understanding of crisis allows ministers to care for people experiencing a wide range of troubling events, because certain common elements generally exist regardless of the precipitator. For the purposes of analysis, these characteristics will be identified and discussed briefly.

Previous Crises

Everyone has experienced a series of normal developmental crises in her or his life. Most have also experienced situational crises. In both cases they probably exhibited patterns of behavior that are common to all people in crisis.

The state of crisis had been assumed clinically but never demonstrated scientifically until crisis intervention theorist Howard Halpern set out to test the hypothesis that "crisis behavior would occur in individuals in crisis situations more significantly than in individuals in noncrisis situations" (1973, 344). Such behaviors included tiredness and exhaustion, helplessness, immobilization, confusion, physical symptoms, anxiety, disorganization of family relationships, and disorganization in social activities. Halpern tested four typical groups of people whom one might expect to be in crisis: divorced persons, students seeking counsel at a mental health clinic, people in bereavement, and individuals entering mental hospitals. He compared them with a control group of persons who had not recently experienced any emotionally hazardous event. The testing and validation of this hypothesis may seem obvious and even unnecessary, but, as Halpern states, "Were this hypothesis not validated, the concept 'crisis' would be meaningless when applied to individuals because their behavior could not be differentiated from that of any individual selected from a noncrisis population."

Crisis behavior occurred significantly more often among people in the test group than among those in the control group. At the same time, Halpern's study found a lack of significant difference among the various types of crisis-precipitating events. No matter what precipitated the crisis, the pattern of response was very much the same. This similarity suggests a considerable commonality in the behavior of people who are in crisis, although what initiated the crisis may be quite diverse. Thus, studying and practicing crisis intervention methods reduces the need to reinvent the wheel with each new precipitating event. Of course, every crisis is unique in a number of respects. Nevertheless, when someone in crisis comes to a minister, the minister can be reasonably sure that the person in crisis will exhibit a particular set of feelings, ways of acting, and thought patterns—and also will have experienced them (to some degree) at an earlier time and place.

Crises as Normative

Again, crisis is not a sign of mental illness but a normal human reaction to an emotionally hazardous situation. In physical disasters, such as hurricanes or earthquakes, no one is surprised to see families or individuals with extreme emotional disturbance. Yet when the precipitator of the crisis is not environmental but emotional or relational, such as bereavement or divorce or a severe disappointment, a stigma tends to be attached to resulting aberrations in behavior. In such situations the affected persons may even be labeled "mentally ill."

Frank Pittman, a family therapist, believes that when helpers encounter a family in crisis they "may find the family disorganized, nonfunctional, directionless, battling over long-dead issues" (1987, 4). He goes on to suggest that helpers may judge the family "far sicker than it is, assume the revived conflicts to be the real issues, and overlook the stress entirely." It is important to underscore that conflict and unhappiness are not necessarily synonymous with mental illness. In fact, in a bad situation, the existence of such conflict and unhappiness is more a sign of health than of illness. For example, a person who does not grieve the death of someone close is more to be suspected of emotional ill health than one who weeps for several weeks or even years afterward.

It must be noted, however, that although persons in crisis are not necessarily mentally ill, they may experience remarkably strong emotional reactions such as anxiety, depression, tension, panic, a personal and social sense of confusion and chaos, feelings of loss, helplessness, hopelessness, and disorganization. The emotional pain even can lead to more serious mental and emotional distress if it is not resolved adaptively.

Crisis Precipitators

We have seen that crises are usually precipitated by an outside precipitator or emotional hazard such as death, divorce, or job loss; these precipitators are always situational and frequently interpersonal in nature.

Halpern's study indicated no significant difference in the quality of the disturbance occasioned by the various precipitators. Nevertheless, some crisis precipitators (such as the death of a spouse) generally stimulate a greater degree of distress than others (such as the birth of a premature child). The extent and duration of the disturbance may be less in some of these secondary crises, but the quality of "being upset" will still manifest itself in a manner similar to cases of more severe crisis precipitators.

The precipitator of a crisis is usually one catastrophic event (like the death of a spouse), but it may also be the accumulation of a series of events. Individuals may weather a series of storms until one final event sends them crashing into the rocks. This final event may not seem like much of a precipitator to the helper (for example, a minor automobile accident with no physical injuries), but it is the proverbial straw that breaks the camel's back. People who apparently have coped well with a series of difficult events suddenly find themselves so exhausted that they cannot deal with one more problem. All their coping resources are spent and they are thrown into crisis.

Many authors who address the causes of emotional problems, such as those associated with divorce, tend to be overly simplistic. Clearly, not all divorced people experience the tumultuous feelings that these writers usually describe. Yet in crisis intervention this focus on the precipitator is critical. It is essential for both the minister and the crisis sufferer to identify the precipitating event.

In some situations, the precipitator is not readily recognizable to the person in distress. For example, a fifty-six-year-old man who went to his family doctor with stomach cramps and depression did not recognize any connection between the pain and his recent discovery that his son was addicted to online pornography and was in trouble with the law. Once the precipitator was uncovered, it became the object of the doctor's efforts to reduce the man's physical symptoms. "The crisis intervener is content . . . to deal primarily with precipitating causes. If someone is shaking with anxiety after an earthquake, one deals with the precipitant of the anxiety and is content to mollify or reduce the intensity of the symptom which resulted from the event" (Shneidman 1973, 10).

The Appraisal of a Threat

The precipitator and the crisis as such have no direct cause-and-effect relationship. In the face of an identical situation, one individual or family will appraise it as emotionally hazardous and experience a crisis, while another will not see it as an acute threat. When the aforementioned mine shut down, the Pulaskis responded quickly and well to the potential emotional hazard and never experienced a crisis. The same event sent shock waves through the Daniels' household. One family carried on with equanimity, while the other family was nearly destroyed.

People's appraisals of emotionally hazardous situations, therefore, greatly determine whether a crisis will occur, and, if so, how serious it will become. Some precipitators have built within them an almost automatic crisis response. Heart attack, unexpected divorce, positive diagnosis of HIV, and death of a child or spouse are all precipitators that almost everyone sees as a serious threat.

For a crisis to develop, a serious threat to self or family has to be perceived—a threat grievous enough to cause disruption of what individuals value most. (I spoke of this factor in connection with the second of the four elements in the development of a crisis.)

During a crisis, people's mental circuits become overloaded. They see the threat as incompatible with their pre-crisis pattern of thinking about themselves or their world. This overload of incompatible information, sometimes called "cognitive dissonance," interferes with usual ways of planning and carrying out effective actions. The cognitive dissonance, which results from people's appraisal of the threat inherent in an event (learning that one has terminal cancer, for example), leads them first to try old and then new and different ways of eradicating the confusing feelings. Some individuals will respond adaptively and others will not. This is obvious to veterans of wartime experience; in a grisly battle some soldiers mature and become healthier mentally as a result of the experience; others fall apart, panic, desert, or break down. Post-traumatic stress disorder (PTSD) results. Few remain unaffected.

Crises and Loss

Most individuals in crisis perceive a loss or are threatened with the loss of something important to them—some source of physical, interpersonal, economical, or emotional well-being. The loss can be of a significant person, a love or dependency relationship, financial support, health, life, a familiar role, a sense of worthfulness, values, or meaning of life. Losses do not necessarily occur only in the form of divorce or death; significant loss can occur when an individual gets a new job or moves to a different part of the country.

When Bill was promoted from machinist to foreman, he gained greater prestige in the eyes of society, better pay, and greater job security. But he lost one of the things that he valued most—his relationship with those who had been his colleagues. Instead of talking and cracking jokes with his equals, he now had to prod subordinates to be more productive, and to report them if they were not. Bill found this role difficult; he was unhappy after his promotion and even talked of quitting. In handling such a loss, clergy who have confronted bereavement many times in their careers can confidently adapt and utilize the same methods with other losses not involving death.

Coping Methods and Resources

A crisis will occur only when early attempts at coping with the threat fail. ("Coping" refers to doing something—even if only choosing to accept one's lot—to resolve the perceived threat in the precipitator.) When habitual coping methods fail, disruption caused by the appraised threat remains or increases. People become immobilized or frantically continue trying those methods that have already proved inadequate for turning back the crisis. People in a crisis often say, "I just don't know what to do," or "I feel so helpless," or "I've tried everything and nothing seems to work." It is this *paralysis* that creates a crisis. Had they been able to use their regular coping methods and deal successfully with the perception of the event, they would not have experienced a crisis.

It is not unusual for people to encounter a number of misfortunes at once. They may have been handling several vexing situations with marginal effectiveness for a prolonged period of time, thus forestalling a crisis. When at last they reach a point of exhaustion, they lack strength to sustain their previously adequate coping resources, and everything falls apart. In such situations the stimulus for the crisis may appear minor to the helper; but a crisis is always of major importance to the person experiencing it, even if the precipitator seems insignificant to others.

The more seriously threatening one's appraisal of an event, the more primitive or regressive one's coping responses will be. Ministers often encounter persons in crisis who manifest considerable dependency and infantile clinging, which tend to repel others and provoke rejection and which can cause isolation.

The greater the number and diversity of coping methods, the more likely individuals will circumvent a crisis, or at least experience a milder crisis than those with poorer coping skills.

Heightened Psychological Accessibility

Heightened psychological accessibility is the most unique and important concept of crisis intervention theory. People in crisis are less defensive, more vulnerable, and more open to change than at other times in their lives. In families the boundaries are loosened, which helps ministers "or anyone else to enter and influence the way the system operates. Rules and roles become confused. Both expectations and prohibitions are relaxed" (Pittman 1987, 4). This heightened accessibility has obvious and important implications when it comes to helping a person in crisis. As Gerald Caplan, one of the early crisis intervention theorists, has stated, "A relatively minor force, acting for a relatively short time, can switch the whole balance to one side or the other—to the side of mental health or to the side of mental ill-health" (1964, 293). Thus, a crisis can be a turning point in a person's emotional, mental, and spiritual health.

In his crisis research, Halpern validated Caplan's argument that people in crisis are more open to intervention of any kind, and he verified their heightened psychological accessibility. He found that those in crisis are less prone to protect themselves and are more open to outside help and assistance toward change.

The period of heightened psychological accessibility generally peaks quickly and lasts only briefly, usually a few days or weeks. Then a restoration of pre-crisis equilibrium occurs. (The restoration of equilibrium is not to be confused with the complete resolution of the problem that initially caused the crisis. For example, the heightened psychological accessibility of one who has been raped may last for only a week, but the scars of the abuse can remain for a lifetime.) When ministers do not establish a relationship quickly—for example, spending too much time gathering information—persons in crisis will move beyond the point of heightened accessibility. More time and effort will be required later than would have been necessary during the time of crisis.

One way to explain this period of heightened psychological accessibility is to use Morley's diagram of a crisis (1970). In diagram 2 the triangle represents an individual who is not in crisis. This person is fairly stable:

Diagram 2

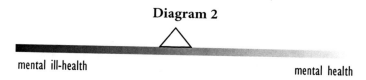

mental ill-health   mental health

One of the sides of the triangle is firmly planted on a continuum between mental health and mental ill-health. People are mostly stable and predictable when not in crisis and therefore are less open to change. A good degree of stability is needed in order to live a normal life.

Diagram 3

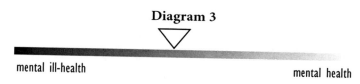

mental ill-health   mental health

Diagram 3 illustrates a person who is in crisis, indicated by the triangle that is tipped up on end. Here the person is in a state of being upset, or of cognitive dissonance. Much less of the personality is firmly planted on the line between mental health and mental ill-health. The individual wants to reestablish stability and is therefore susceptible to any influence from the inside or outside that will bring comfort and aid in resolving the crisis. Thus, with minimal effort, ministers, mental health professionals, or family members may exert a maximum amount of helping leverage on the individual.

In my book *Suicide and Grief* (Stone 1972, 69–70), I pointed out that "during the period of crisis, with individuals' greater susceptibility to change, less counseling is required to aid them toward effective resolution of their problems. Often, the difficulty is that we do not help soon enough. Once the crisis stage is past, it takes more leverage to bring change because the 'triangle' is back on its base." The brief period when the triangle is tipped up is so significant because of the emotional intensity, the cognitive dissonance, the loosened boundaries, and the heightened vulnerability. Successful crisis intervention makes maximum use of the heightened psychological accessibility of individuals and families in crisis. All crisis caregiving needs to start from this basic principle.

Crisis as a Danger and Opportunity

Crisis resolution can be for better or for worse. Even though people may go through considerable emotional pain during a crisis, it can become a positive experience and a chance for growth and maturation. To let a crisis go by without learning from it is to waste a valuable opportunity.

Most ministers have seen both adaptive and unadaptive reactions among the bereaved. I recall Agatha, a thirty-seven-year-old woman in Los Angeles who stated that although she wished her husband had not died and would not like to go through the grief again, she felt she was a better person, more "alive," as a result of the experience. Before his death she was living in a rut, but since then she had increasingly valued her relationships with other people and with God. She had gained meaning in her life. She still grieved, yet she felt stronger than ever emotionally.

In sad contrast to Agatha is Horace, a fifty-seven-year-old man whom I counseled several times. Since his wife's death ten years ago he had lived under a cloud. He was chronically depressed and exhausted, and twice had entered a mental hospital, totally out of touch with reality. Horace thought about his late wife obsessively and kept several rooms of their home exactly as they were before she died. Unlike Agatha, who coped successfully with her crisis, Horace responded to the death of his wife in a most unadaptive way.

A history of successful resolution of past crises increases the chances of successfully resolving each new one. In the cases of Agatha and Horace, the vastly different reactions to bereavement were somewhat dependent upon how they dealt with previous crises in their lives. The cumulative effect of unresolved problems from the past can combine with new crises to make them even harder to resolve. Agatha had weathered a number of earlier, less serious crises, and they better prepared her to cope with what is for most people the worst crisis precipitator they will face. Horace had a history of adapting poorly to stressful situations prior to the death of his wife, especially to his mother's death. In his case the triangle tipped toward danger, while for Agatha it became an opportunity.

Crises of Religious Values

Paul Tillich defined pastoral care as a "helping encounter in the dimension of ultimate concern" (quoted in Clinebell 1984, 67). Besides causing upheaval in an individual's emotional, physical, and intellectual life, a crisis also can upset a person's values and sense of meaning. One encounters the basic contradiction between infinite aspirations and finite possibilities (Gerkin 1987). Every crisis at its core raises issues of faith, and asks questions such as: What is the meaning of life? Is it worth the pain to continue living? Did I do the right thing? Why did this happen to me? Why does God allow me to suffer? Can I ever trust anyone again? Asking these questions requires openness to the vulnerability of an unknowable future; they require the making of faith choices. "Hope that is seen is not hope. For who hopes for what is seen? But if we hope for what we do not see, we wait for it with patience" (Rom. 8:24-25).

Ministers or counselors who deal with the emotional, physical, or intellectual life and ignore the spiritual core of crises are not responding to the whole person. During crises, because of their heightened psychological accessibility, people may be especially receptive to issues of faith if they are sensitively portrayed.

Conversely, during a crisis, upstanding members of a congregation may question in their faith what they had previously affirmed. The minister needs to remain emotionally with them at such times. The helper's sensitivity and ministry of presence can aid them in weathering their uncertainty (Stone 1996).

Changing the Situation

Situational aspects frequently are factors in sustaining a crisis; altering the environment often can change the course of a crisis positively.

Alicia Brown, a twenty-nine-year-old Philadelphian whose husband had abandoned her five weeks before she sought help, was the mother of four children from two to eight years old. Alicia's crisis was precipitated when the utility companies turned off her electricity and gas in the middle of winter, and the landlord, after repeated requests for payment of back rent, gave her two days to come up with the back rent or be put out in the street.

Alicia tried in vain for one whole day to borrow the money she needed. Finally she walked into a downtown church and told the minister her situation. Within twenty-four hours the minister was able to find Alicia another apartment, arrange for several church members to help her move, and put her in touch with a social worker who would help her obtain money and food for herself and her children.

Although she would have had legal recourse against her previous landlord, it would have been temporary at best. The alteration of her environmental situation—moving to another (nicer) apartment and receiving some money and food—resolved Alicia's immediate crisis. She had other problems, to be sure. The immensity of the immediate problem had paralyzed her so that she was not able to do anything—even basic things like feeding her children. But removing a couple of basic obstacles in the life of her family moved her to a place where she could start addressing her other difficulties one at a time. What is more, because of the involvement of the church, she now had a new set of relationships that could sustain her as she moved forward with her life.

Need for Positive Relationships

People in crisis often tend to pull away from the very interpersonal relationships that they need more than ever—whether out of embarrassment, an instinct to be alone and lick one's wounds, confusion about what to do, or a desire to hide the crisis from others. Positive interpersonal relationships foster adaptive crisis resolution.

A significant factor in the resolution of Alicia's crisis was her willingness to seek help from others. A troubled person is not an isolated individual but an interacting member of a social system. In crisis intervention the minister needs to realize that, for instance, if a woman has lost her job, the crisis may involve not only her but her husband and children as well. Persons in crisis need other caring people around them. (In this regard, couples in the process of divorce are particularly needy because they are sometimes treated as emotional lepers at a time when they require friends and relatives more than ever.) A lack of valuable interpersonal relationships will almost certainly heighten the suffering of persons in crisis.

Crisis Ministry as the Priesthood of All Believers

Intervention in crises is not the exclusive domain of clergy and mental health professionals. The entire priesthood of believers is called to a ministry of caring for the neighbor. The empathy, warmth, and concern of laypersons and significant others may be both necessary and sufficient in the resolution of a crisis. Pastors are not offering optimal care when, hearing of a crisis, they don their white hats, mount their steeds, and charge to the rescue—ignoring the considerable assistance lay ministers have to offer. Effective crisis intervention caregiving by clergy often means enabling others to care for those in crisis. In a study of the members of a large church who experienced a crisis, the research team noted that in many instances one of the most significant factors that helped a family weather a crisis was the care, concern, and prayers of other members of the church (Stone et al. 2003; Stone et al. 2004; this is discussed in greater detail in chapter 6).

People's Expectations

All persons who come for help have a particular set of expectations, the fulfillment of which is one of the most important factors in arriving at a positive outcome. In some forms of traditional counseling, psychotherapists endeavor to go beneath the original problem and expectations of clients to what they hypothesize are deeper underlying ones. This approach may be valuable in long-term therapy; however, in crisis intervention it is important, wherever possible, to work toward the fulfillment of people's stated goals. The minister's task is to assist them in discerning exactly what they expect to achieve (the goal) and then to help them reach it (discussed in greater detail in chapter 3 and in Stone 1994 and Stone 2001).

Equipped with a basic understanding of the dynamics and characteristics of crisis, ministers can begin to utilize these insights to ease the distress of people coming to them for help. They can view the singularity of each individual human situation in balance with the knowledge of experiences common to all who find themselves in crises, facilitating an orderly and tested approach to the resolution of these boundary experiences.

3

A DESIGN FOR INTERVENTION

Hector Martinez called his pastor at 11:45 P.M. Thursday night. He and his wife had fought again, and she wanted a divorce. Pastor Cole knew that Hector, twenty-nine, and Donna, twenty-seven, had been having trouble for the six years they had been married, though whenever he visited them in their home they always acted the part of the happily married couple. Hector did not want a divorce.

Hector asked Pastor Cole to come immediately, but the pastor, determining that there was no immediate physical danger, set up an appointment for the next morning at his office. When they arrived late Donna stated, "I only came because he wanted me to. I've made up my mind: I'm going to get a divorce and not you or anybody else can change my mind." She felt their relationship was beyond help.

Hector said the problem was that she wanted a divorce. Donna said the problem was Hector and everything he did. After the session, Pastor Cole arranged to see the couple again three days later. He telephoned their home several times between sessions without reaching either of them.

At the appointed hour Hector showed up alone, saying that Donna had forced him out of the house and he was staying at his brother's place. He cried through most of the session. All he could think about was his tremendous loss, and all he wanted out of counseling was to get back his wife. "There is nothing left in life anymore without her," Hector said. "If she doesn't come back, I'm going to kill myself."

How might this situation be handled? Is there any hope for the marriage? What would be the best way to approach Hector Martinez's talk of suicide?

These questions deserve answers as surely as Hector needed immediate help. First, though, it would be useful to look at a framework for responding—a design for pastoral crisis intervention. The crisis intervention methods described in this chapter take full advantage of the healing forces that already exist in people like Hector (especially those in crisis who seem lacking in resources). They also exploit distinctive opportunities for caring that are inherent in the church.

ADVANTAGES OF CRISIS INTERVENTION METHODS

Crisis-intervention methods have several advantages over traditional counseling practice in times of a crisis such as the one Hector Martinez experienced. First, crisis intervention methods are designed specifically to deal with crisis and not with other mental, emotional, or spiritual problems. Just as some methods are especially effective with autistic children, and others with chronic depressive individuals, crisis intervention methods have been designed to take advantage of the unique aspects of a crisis and to use the heightened psychological accessibility to its full benefit.

Second, clergy sometimes encounter backlash from people with whom they have had long-term, in-depth counseling relationships. Because crisis intervention is short-term in nature and focuses on immediate problem solving, parishioners need not fear that the minister will delve into all the dark nooks and crannies of their psyches; they are less likely to resent their pastor or leave the church later, out of embarrassment. (Although it can still happen.)

Third, crisis intervention is effective with individuals from a wide range of cultural and socioeconomic groups. According to Gerald Jacobson (1965, 214–15), any assistance in which the helper and the one seeking help are "psychosocial strangers must, at least at first, minimize the differences between the persons involved and maximize what unites them. . . . The more acute the crisis, the less the sense of strangeness, even with patients and therapists widely divergent in social background or age." Especially among poorer people, a demand for immediate and concrete action rather than delaying gratification for the sake of long-term mental health goals is common. Crisis intervention is geared to this need.

Fourth, as a brief method of pastoral care and counseling, crisis intervention does not use up large periods of the pastor's time. Because a crisis's duration is at most six weeks (see chapter 2), the minister will not face a long-term time commitment.

Finally, crisis intervention is a method of pastoral care that laypersons in the congregation can practice. Although it is most effective with training and supervised practice, it is not necessary to undergo years of training in psychodynamics, pathology, and analysis in order to be a competent crisis intervener.

PREPARING TO COUNSEL DURING CRISES

Ministers need to prepare themselves on a number of levels to deal with crucial situations. They cannot overlook their own personal issues that may arise when they encounter crisis situations. The following are some personal preparations I have found valuable.

First, I have to reflect on the care that I offer and the motives behind my helping acts—to recognize that at times I get in the way. If a person's crisis is similar to one I experienced recently, or never completely resolved, my ability to help may be impaired. At such times I need help in the form of case consultation or referral, discussed at the end of this chapter. I need to know my own limitations in order to care effectively for others. To give a hypothetical example: if Pastor Cole had had serious, unresolved marital problems of his own when Hector came to him for help, it could have compromised the quality of care for Hector and his wife. (The opposite is also true; successful resolution of one's own divorce or marital crisis might lead to greater wisdom and compassion for Hector and Donna.)

Second, I must prepare to accept failure. Definitions of success and failure are elusive, but sometimes, no matter how I rationalize it, I feel that I have failed. True, every counselor has made mistakes; but it is also true that people sometimes refuse help. Because all change is experienced as loss, people in crisis will naturally have mixed feelings about making changes in their lives, and their ambivalence may affect the outcome of any attempt at intervention.

Third, I have to be sensitive to expectations others have of me as a pastor and to the role they assign me, which may derive from their previous experiences with a minister. Most people do not know how to act in counseling. Their impressions largely reflect stereotypes in literature, media, even comic strips. I can still see the startled look on the face of a late-middle-aged woman who first saw a youngish-looking pastoral counselor without a tie or coat and exclaimed, "You're not *Doctor* Stone, are you?" (The woman later explained that she had expected me to be fifty, gray, and bearded. Some thirty-five years later, I seem to have grown into her stereotype.) Some people think that ministers and counselors can wave a magic wand and solve any problem. The magic may occasionally work in the helper's favor—but never for long. Pastoral caregivers need to be aware of these expectations and be prepared to discuss them if they interfere with the care process.

Fourth, I need to prepare for pastoral crisis intervention by conditioning and improving my ability to cope with negative feelings—anger, sarcasm, belittlement—directed toward me. During my freshman year in college, I was canvassing for a local inner-city church in Minneapolis. We were instructed to ask a few basic questions and then be ready to sit and talk with anyone who requested it. At one apartment I encountered a man in his forties who gruffly invited me in. After I had settled myself and asked five or six questions about his church affiliation, he said, "You're a Christian; I have a question for you. My son was killed—run over by a car two weeks ago. Why did God do that? Why did God allow it to happen?" He proceeded to castigate me for the hypocrisy of Christians, the foolishness of religion, and the fact that I had no answers to his questions. I agonized through his angry words and gestures, frozen to my chair with fear. If he had not been standing between me and the door, I would have fled. After what seemed like an eternity but was probably only a few minutes, he broke down and cried: "You're the first one who has listened to me." Although I can't take the credit, my somewhat captive listening ear gave him a much-needed opportunity to express feelings about his son's death.

Sometimes we have to wade through the murky waters of black and angry emotions before reaching some solid ground for intervention. I am not suggesting that caregivers become emotional whipping posts. However, people in crisis sometimes share things that they later regret telling. Helpers can expect to give generously of themselves, stay up late, miss an occasional day off—and later receive no thanks or even experience hostility from the recipient of their care.

Another danger I must prepare for is the possibility of going into a crisis myself while caring for others—thus losing the ability to relate in a calm and relaxed manner, and to see alternative solutions to a problem. Ministers react differently to the anxiety of a crisis. Some are tempted to talk too much or fail to listen closely, others quote Scripture or authoritarian dictates, and still others become paralyzed. These, of course, are reflexive responses; we can do better. Whatever response anxiety produces, be aware of it and develop strategies to circumvent it. The best course when sensing the onset of a crisis-like state in yourself is to invite another capable minister or mental health worker to share the burden for the case (this is *essential* when a person is suicidal) or by referring the case to another source of help. I always have found that by sharing a troubling situation with at least one other person I give myself a chance to release my own anxieties and get another perspective on the crisis.

One prerequisite for pastoral crisis intervention is necessary for all pastoral-care work: to care genuinely for the person in crisis. Becoming so concerned with one's role, intervention techniques, or other personal responsibilities that one loses sight of the mission to love others might cause a caregiver to miss seeing the person in crisis as infinitely worthful. I have found that holding the person in prayer has always helped me to focus on the other's needs rather than my own issues. This aspect of preparation may seem so obvious that it need not be mentioned, but sometimes it is remarkably easy for counselees to become cases, problems, or challenges rather than unique and precious human beings.

THE A-B-C METHOD OF CRISIS INTERVENTION

The goal of crisis counseling is to help persons in crisis regain at least their pre-crisis level of functioning, and (one hopes) to grow to even higher levels. The first step toward this goal is to determine if a crisis really exists. Switzer (1986, 41) believes that this can be ascertained by answering three questions: "(1) Has there been a recent (within a few weeks) onset of the troublesome feelings and/or behavior? (2) Have they tended to grow progressively worse? (3) Can the time of onset be linked with some external event, some change in the person's life situation?" If the answer to all three questions is yes, then a crisis most likely exists.

The model of crisis intervention offered here is my adaptation of the A-B-C method first formulated by psychiatrist Warren L. Jones (1968, 87), as a method for helping people in crisis. (His method was further developed and confirmed by Howard Cline-bell and David Switzer and influenced by such theorists as Robert Carkhuff and Allen Ivey.)

The A-B-C method of pastoral crisis intervention has three elements: (A) *A*chieve contact with the person; (B) *B*oil down the problem to its essentials; and (C) *C*ope actively with the problem. This method does not require a linear progression from A to B to C; two or three steps can and frequently do occur at the same time.

Achieving Contact with the Person in Crisis

The initial step for helping individuals in crisis is to achieve contact—in other words, to establish an empathetic relationship. If a relationship already exists, this can speed the initial phase of crisis intervention. A solid, supportive relationship not only serves to help troubled people to feel comfortable but also becomes the means through which the minister can move them from expressing their emotions to taking action. The relationship is not the goal of crisis intervention, but, rather, the basis upon which the care process grows toward crisis resolution.

A relationship of trust and empathy is no less important in crisis intervention than in other forms of counseling or pastoral care, but (because persons in crisis are usually less defensive than normal) it may come about with a smaller amount of time and effort. In establishing relationships, crisis intervention helpers use the basic relation-building skills of attending behaviors and listening.

Attending Behaviors. Attending behaviors are the minister's physical, nonverbal acts that communicate interest and concern and help produce a relaxed and comfortable environment for people. They are a way of saying "I care about you." A variety of actions serve this function.

One attending behavior valuable in the development of a relationship is *symbolic nourishing*. Perhaps the first way we experience the care of another is nursing at our mother's breast or being held and fed by either parent. From infancy onward, one of the simplest and most effective ways in which we perceive the concern and care of others is through actual and symbolic nourishment with food and drink. Delivering a coffee cake or a cooked meal to a bereaved family is an example of this attending behavior. Similarly, providing a comfortable, relaxed environment and a cup of coffee or a glass of water demonstrates our concern.

Physical posture (sometimes called body language) also can communicate interest and readiness to respond. The most helpful posture is to face people and lean forward slightly. Consider your own natural body language; when you are deeply interested in what someone is saying, you often move to the edge of your chair to hear better. Such a move closes the physical distance and signals active interest. (My wife has often told students who are not very interested in a subject that they should *pretend* to be fascinated. Inevitably, the physical postures required for pretending interest result in real interest.)

Another way that people experience care and concern from earliest infancy is by *being held and touched* by parents, relatives, friends, and babysitters. The need for touch continues into adulthood. Holding the hand of a person in grief, touching the shoulder of one who is upset, or even a handshake gently communicate our concern through touch. The great benefit of touch is that it can transmit caring feelings when words are impossible; most pastors have experienced these moments of contact at the bedside of someone who is dying. Be cautioned, however, that appropriate public behavior such as hugging during the Passing of the Peace or after worship is not appropriate in an ongoing, private caregiving situation. All attending behaviors, especially touching, must be offered only when the person will receive them positively. Some people object to being touched in any way. A person of the opposite gender may interpret touching as a sexual gesture. The evening paper and TV news programs are full of examples of touching gone too far. When using this attending behavior the pastoral caregiver must observe proper boundaries with those in distress

Looking into the eyes of a troubled person is one of the most powerful attending behaviors for communicating concern. Some people cannot verbalize without this eye contact. One day, when I was talking with a professor in her classroom, she turned away to wipe off the blackboard; as she did so I stopped talking without noticing it. She turned back to me and remarked, "You need eye contact, don't you?" The required amount of eye contact varies from individual to individual. People who get too much eye contact will show their discomfort by looking away, pulling back in their chair, or closing their eyes. A few will share their discomfort verbally. If the amount of eye contact is too brief, however, people may be reluctant to share their problems and feelings in more than a superficial manner—if they share them at all.

Creating an environment is an attending behavior. The room in which the caregiver receives people in distress ought to communicate calmness, confidentiality, and openness. Ideally, both the caregiver and the person seeking help should sit in comfortable chairs of equal height, facing each other. Doors to the room can be shut or slightly ajar. Noises from the outside cannot intrude because the person needs to be confident that no one can overhear the conversation. Many pastors are now installing glass doors to their office in order to address concerns about inappropriate behavior. If the room is reasonably in order, and the temperature and lighting are at comfortable levels, the individual will relax more.

The environment will not always be ideal; care can be offered in a kitchen, walking down a street, or standing in an emergency ward. Best is a relaxed area that is safe and conducive to private conversation. Move from the kitchen to a living room or den; leave the street for a quiet coffee shop; step out of the hospital waiting room and into the quiet of the chapel. The setting in which listening occurs can greatly affect the troubled person's openness to caring intervention.

Listening. The second important skill in establishing a relationship is listening, which in some respects might also be considered an attending behavior. Giving full and undivided attention to what persons in crisis are saying communicates caring and concern. To quote Dietrich Bonhoeffer (1978, 97):

> The first service that one owes to others in the fellowship consists in listening to them. Just as love of God begins with listening to His Word, so the beginning of love for [others] is learning to listen to them. It is God's love for us that He not only gives us His Word but also lends us His ear. So it is His work that we do for [others] when we learn to listen to them. Christians, especially ministers, so often think they must always contribute something when they are in the company of others, that this is

the one service they have to render. They forget that listening can be a greater service than speaking.

Bonhoeffer captured an important attitude of the Christian life: *listening* to God and to neighbor. The following are some suggestions for responsive listening, which is vital in crisis intervention.

Outside distractions, such as street noise, radios, or phone calls, can interrupt an important revelation. Of course these distractions should be avoided or minimized; but inner distractions, such as thinking about your to-do list, can also impede listening. People usually sense such inner distance and consequently avoid revealing much about themselves.

Inappropriate attending behaviors—laughing (even sympathetically) as the other breaks into tears—can also sabotage self-disclosure. When the listener's behaviors are not congruent with the feelings being expressed, the person may perceive that she or he is not being heard—or worse, being mocked—and as a result may talk less freely. As Paul wrote, "Rejoice with those who rejoice, weep with those who weep" (Rom. 12:15).

Listening needs to focus on the presenting problem and the precipitator of the crisis. How does the person in crisis perceive the emotionally hazardous situation? What coping methods and resources have been used to deal with the crisis? Sensing how this person experiences the stress of the crisis is important because in step B, boiling down, the person needs help in focusing on just that: what the crisis means to him or her personally.

Temporarily suspending all judgments allows the individual to express his or her emotions. Especially in the early phases of a relationship, criticism—or evaluations that are taken as such—can make the person reticent to continue sharing; many will shut down altogether in the face of perceived judgment. In pastoral care judgment may sometimes be called for, but not until a solid relationship is established and almost never while the person is in a crisis state.

Individuals in crisis sometimes have difficulty saying clearly what they want to express; helpers need to be patient. In the confusion of a crisis, people's mental processes are not functioning normally. They may experience pain so profound that they have difficulty verbalizing it. For example, how can one express in words the depth of grief felt immediately after the death of someone close? At first it is valuable to allow long pauses before responding to what is said. Most beginning crisis interveners are overly anxious about filling in these silences; as a result, instead of listening, they are busy figuring out what to say next.

Ministers need to attend to important themes as a person speaks about the crisis. Usually people state such themes (such as forgiveness, resentment, self-doubt, fear) repeatedly or with great intensity. These recurring themes will be valuable clues in helping people to focus on the essence of their distress.

Time is of the essence. In crisis intervention it is important early on to let people know that they need to move quickly toward goals and resolution. The key is to narrow the focus of communication by selectively reinforcing those topics that are related to the crisis and by withholding response to those that are irrelevant. It is best to allow people considerable freedom in the first one-third to one-half of the initial interview, but thereafter increasingly to focus the conversation on the actual crisis. Often it is enough to say, "That sounds like something important that we should address, but it doesn't seem directly related to your present problem. As soon as we have resolved this crisis we can return to it."

Without realizing it, pastoral caregivers may encourage a return to ineffective childhood behaviors—by allowing rambling, unfocused conversation or talk that mainly focuses on past events; by not encouraging people to use their own resources of self-observation, self-restraint, and self-responsibility; by allowing them to detach from their feelings without calling them back to awareness; or by permitting anything to keep them from focusing on the immediate crisis.

Psychotherapists are trained to avoid taking too much responsibility in counseling, but the crisis helper sometimes needs to be active and assertive (even breaking confidentiality in rare but necessary cases such as threats of suicide or violence) in order to make decisions for those who are unable to handle the decision-making process on their own. Such persons need a crisis intervener who does more than reflect feelings or offer passive support. In other words, it is the caregiver's task to take responsibility, but only to the extent it is needed. As Thomas Rusk (1971, 251) puts it, "Do

for others that which they cannot do for themselves, and no more." I would add that as soon as they are able to handle things on their own *stop* doing for them.

While establishing the relationship, caregivers should communicate as much as possible their own self-confidence, calmness, stability, and willingness to take an active role. A troubled individual, particularly in crisis, initially may be unable to act or decide or take any responsibility alone, and needs to sense these strengths within the pastoral caregiver. Attending and listening communicates a genuine love and a depth of involvement and caring.

Boiling Down the Problem to Its Essentials

The second step of the A-B-C method of crisis intervention involves reducing the problem to its essential elements. This step requires responding to people in crisis in such a way that they can define in their own minds what has happened, what they are feeling, and why. The boiling-down phase calls upon the helper's skills of responding and focusing.

Responding. Responding is one of the basic dimensions of all human interchange; communication, verbal or nonverbal, is not complete until there is response. Helpers have already begun responding to persons in crisis while achieving contact (A), but during the boiling-down phase (B) helpers will have fewer and shorter periods of only listening.

To go beyond attending and listening and to begin boiling down the problem to its essentials, it is necessary to distinguish between facilitative and nonfacilitative ways of responding. The following are *not* helpful ways of responding to those in crisis.

One of the quickest ways to miss the pain of others and to leave them feeling unheard is to offer *quick advice*. For example, making suggestions only ten minutes after a person starts talking does not take seriously what the other has to say or the complexity of the issues involved. Furthermore, advice offered before a solid relationship has been established will probably go unheeded. Only after a caring relationship has been founded and alternative strategies of action have been explored are tentative offerings of advice helpful.

Likewise, *false assurances* accomplish nothing. Telling a wife whose husband has just left her, "I'm sure he'll come back," or a person facing exploratory surgery, "Everything is going to be just fine," assumes a knowledge you do not possess. Most people reject such statements as insincere. They may even mumble, "How do you know?" It is desirable to support an individual emotionally and to reassure him or her realistically; it is inauthentic and inappropriate to promise what is impossible to predict.

Well-meaning but ineffectual helpers sometimes summarize complex problems in the form of *bromides,* such as "God helps those who help themselves"; "If you make your bed, you have to lie in it"; "A fellow ought to go out and sow some wild oats before he settles down." Bromides contain some kernels of truth but are not very personal or helpful. The caregiver's responses ought to be specific, clear, and individually tailored to the issues about which the troubled person is talking. The greater the specificity of a response, the greater the applicability of the help offered.

The number of *questions* posed to people in crisis should be kept to a minimum because questions tend to put people on the spot and narrow their range of expression. This is especially true of closed-ended queries ("How old are you?" "Did you want to marry him in the first place?" "How many years did you go together?" "Did you love her?") that call only for a word or a phrase reply and do not allow others to tell their own stories in their own ways. Open-ended questions are more effective: "How have you felt recently about your husband?" "What are your concerns about this operation?" "What is it like at home now that your last daughter has moved out?" "Tell me about . . ."

Judgmental pronouncements ("That's dumb!"; "You were foolish to tell your husband about your affair"; "A Christian should not smoke.") are apt to do more harm than good. God's love is meted out in both judgment and grace, and sometimes it is essential for Christians not to remain morally neutral; however, at the beginning of a helping relationship, passing judgment ignores the complexities of the troubled person's problems. After a relationship is well established and considerable listening has occurred, it is appropriate to voice a personal understanding of the ethics of a given situation—as long as this statement remains tentative and

gentle, allowing the other to sense the compassion and hear the concern that prompts such a witness.

Responses should focus directly on what the person says and never slide into analysis of the person. Statements like "That's probably because of the harsh treatment your mother gave you" or "You're doing that because of your resentment toward women" are examples of unhelpful analytical responses. The minister should let each individual draw his or her own conclusions.

Debating or arguing with a person who is experiencing a crisis usually creates distance rather than closeness. The caregiver needs to respect the right of persons to maintain their own, different views by neither criticizing nor belittling those persons or their views.

Finally, although sharing personal struggles and joys as one finite human being with another can be effective, using the relationship as a place to *seek release* is not proper. The caregiver should get help, if needed, from others.

Probably the best way to develop effective, facilitative responding skills is to learn mirroring, or reflecting back in a sentence or two the essence of what the other person has shared ("I hear you saying you feel . . ."). In establishing a relationship it is best to respond at first primarily to feelings. As the relationship develops, both feelings and content become increasingly important because the two together reveal the meaning of what is being expressed. For example: "I hear you saying you feel low" reflects a feeling (sad or depressed), whereas "since you lost your job" reflects content (being fired). Only when the two are viewed together is the full meaning apparent. The cause of the depression is recognized when the content is added—the loss of the job. The following are additional features of effective response and good feedback.

- *Specificity.* Vague or general responses, such as "You are too aggressive," are hard for the person to use. "You speak loudly and interrupt others" is more to the point, describing behaviors that a person can observe and alter.
- *Using open-ended questions.* Limit the number of questions you ask and make them open ended, requiring more than a simple yes or no answer.
- *Describing rather than evaluating.* Describing a feeling response to something the person has said is better than putting a label

on that statement: "I sense you have reservations about making these changes" rather than "You're stubborn."

- *Responding with immediacy.* It is important to give frequent feedback, at the appropriate time, rather than save it all up for a summarizing conclusion.
- *Brevity.* Limiting most responses to a sentence or two whenever possible is better than lengthy responses.
- *Checking for understanding.* If any uncertainty remains regarding understanding—whether you have understood or been understood correctly—inquire about this. One way to check is to have the other rephrase what he or she heard (that is, mirror back to the caregiver).
- *Pauses.* It is better to allow lapses in conversation when they occur naturally and not to pepper the dialogue with new questions whenever the person takes a breath. Pauses not only allow the individual to reflect on what has been said but also give the carer a chance to formulate responses without using valuable listening time to do so.

Focusing. Individuals often are not fully aware of the precipitating stress and its consequences. The focusing process aims at prompt identification of the nature of the threat, and clarification of the relevant circumstances and conflicts. When the crisis can be defined clearly and the nature of the threat to the person clarified, a plan for its resolution becomes possible; indeed, ideally it would emerge out of the individual's own thinking.

Some individuals in crisis momentarily evade reality, defend themselves against its pain and need encouragement to look clearly at the reality of what has happened. The caregiver creates an environment in which the person feels comfortable enough to confront the crisis and the event that precipitated it. In focusing, the minister needs to be aware of the following: (1) the precipitating event; (2) the loss or threatened loss of something or someone important; (3) the individual's coping methods and resources; and (4) new factors or conditions which may cause his or her traditional methods of coping to fail.

Focusing includes filtering out irrelevant data. Persons in crisis sometimes share meaningless information without knowing it is meaningless. If a person brings up seemingly unrelated material, the minister can try to relate it to the present crisis—or show its irrelevance—with a statement such as, "I wonder how you see this relating to your immediate problem."

Once the situation is accurately assessed, the minister communicates the essence of the dilemma as simply and directly as possible. This communication has been called "consensual formulation." The minister and the individual mutually come to an understanding of what has happened and put it into words. The distressed person is able to move to the next elements of the crisis intervention process: examining alternative methods of dealing with the present crisis, choosing those that seem appropriate, and mobilizing available resources. When it's not possible to arrive at consensual formulation, there is less chance for personal growth and learning from the crisis, even though the crisis may be resolved adaptively.

The development of a consensual formulation can in itself reduce the anxiety level and enhance the self-esteem of the person in crisis. It accomplishes a basic purpose of crisis counseling, namely, to help the person pull out of the tailspin.

Coping Actively with the Problem

In the final stage of the A-B-C method, ministers help those in crisis to evaluate and mobilize their resources, develop a plan of action, and make specific changes directed toward resolving the crisis. The ultimate goal of all helping is *action*—such as making a decision, accepting a loss that cannot be changed, learning a new skill, or finding a job. Thoughtful yet decisive action leads to growth.

Knowing what the problem is but being unable to find a solution is a common difficulty for those in crisis, yet it is useless to boil down the problem if the person does not take action. Each pastoral caregiver requires a systematic problem-solving model (or models) in order to help people weigh alternatives, make decisions, and take the first steps toward problem resolution (Stone 1994; Stone 2001). Problem management methods are based on the assumption that merely communicating about a problem and expressing one's feelings about it are not always sufficient. In some cases the problem persists (for example, the alcoholic wife continues berating her husband whenever she drinks) until the person takes action and begins to make responsible choices.

The minister needs to help those in crisis examine alternative courses of action with which they can take to reshape their lives, and then has to challenge them to act upon one or more of those alternatives. Such problem management usually has five components: establishing goals; taking inventory of resources; formulating alternatives; committing to action; and evaluating.

Establishing Goals. Ideally, at this point in the A-B-C method, the minister has established a relationship, allowed the expression of thoughts and feelings, and helped the person boil down and define the problem. The next task is to establish goals or hoped-for solutions. This task is usually fairly simple, inasmuch as crisis counseling aims only at the removal of symptoms and the achievement of a level of functioning as high as or higher than before.

Changing the focus of helping from negative (problems) to positive (goals or solutions) is the first step. Once some general, long-term goals are stated, it is important to develop specific, short-term, easily attained objectives toward which the problem solving will be aimed. For example, if the problem is that a void was created when a couple's last daughter joined the Air Force and moved to another country, the goal is to find new tasks and meaning now that the nest is empty and only long-distance parenting is required; one objective may be to start up the mail-order business they had talked about for years but never seemed to have time to put into operation.

The goal determines the direction in which the care will proceed and toward which the courses of action will be aimed. It is always best to be as specific as possible in defining goals, and to express them in observable terms. It is far more helpful to establish small and short-term aims, and to attain them, than to set up lofty, long-term goals that may not be reached and will bring disappointment. Most of the useful goals in crisis counseling should be attainable in a matter of weeks.

Taking Inventory of Resources. After the goal has been delineated, ministers will need to help individuals take inventory of their internal and external resources. People in crisis sometimes have trouble reviewing their resources rationally, and the minister may have to take the lead.

Internal resources are those methods of coping that each person has developed and upon which he or she can draw in the face of daily problems. Sometimes people are not aware of their internal resources. The minister needs to point them out by saying, for example: "You say you can't tell people what you feel, but I see you doing a great job of telling your feelings to me." One significant internal resource is the experience of handling past crises. Once again, the minister who previously has shared developmental or situational crises with people is in a good position to help them discover what led to their successful resolution and apply those lessons to their present troubles.

External resources include friends, family, church, community groups, and finances, to name a few. People who are in crisis often pull away from meaningful interpersonal involvement and feel lonely. A relatively modest degree of concern on the part of others often is enough to exert a great deal of positive influence upon those in crisis. The support that a now-lost relationship had offered may be regained through contact with a new significant person or through the strengthening of a preexisting relationship.

Those who are emotionally close to a person in crisis frequently need pastoral care as well. They are under greater-than-normal pressures during the crisis and may themselves require special guidance and support, though not necessarily from the minister. Here an organized program of lay pastoral care, involving people in the congregation who are capable and willing to move into crisis situations and are not frightened by them, can be of great help (Stone 1991).

Individuals in crisis can find additional support in ongoing fellowship or prayer groups within the church (see chapter 6). The worship and occasional services of the church (a funeral service, confession, or an order for the Blessing of a Civil Marriage) may also offer an important resource in a crisis.

Even in the most remote rural area, community resources are probably available in times of crisis. They include counseling agencies, visiting nurses, adult day care, treatment centers, support groups, local business and service organizations, and a host of other supportive activities. Even ordinary people may be marshaled to lend a hand, raise money, give blood, or sit with the bereaved. Individuals who have recently been in counseling are best referred back to the same counselor (one should carefully evaluate protests such as "She didn't help me" before accepting them at face value). People in crisis also may resist listing as resources those whom they feel are unwilling or unable to help. Others often become irritated by the whining, dependency, depression, and helplessness that crises sometimes bring out in people, but they are more likely to mobilize if the minister can help them see the extent of the need and their potential for offering support. Therefore, one task in crisis intervention is to help these significant other individuals care for the troubled person as effectively as possible (discussed in greater detail in chapter 6).

Formulating Alternatives. After developing goals and reviewing resources, the minister and the persons in crisis brainstorm alternative courses of action that might facilitate these goals. The minister encourages them to develop their own alternatives, and both good and bad ideas are included on the list of ideas. The caregiver can jar their thinking by suggesting courses of action they would never have considered. This is not a matter of advice giving but an attempt to broaden the horizons of persons who may still be cognitively constricted and who cannot think of alternatives; in almost every case, the individual personally chooses the course of action to take.

From the list of alternatives, the minister and the person in crisis weed out all irrelevant and unworkable courses of action. For example, the single mother who feels pressured by the responsibilities of home, three children, and a full-time job may not be able to quit her job and stay home. If she has no other means of income, such a course would be impossible even if it were desirable. The person in crisis works with the minister to evaluate the remaining choices; the task is to weigh these options against the individual's personal values (money, free time, job, family). If a particular alternative would violate several of his or her values, it can be eliminated. The man who is having financial problems but places a high value on his work in the church, his free time, and his family, will certainly reject the idea of a second job as a breach of those values.

After weighing courses of action in terms of values, the minister and the counselee consider each course's potential effectiveness.

Will it lead to the chosen goals? After the troubled person has considered the potential effectiveness of each alternative, the minister can step in and share information from his or her own experience, or from the experiences of other counselees (always maintaining confidentiality). For example, a recently divorced man was isolating himself and yet wanted to meet people; I told him that a number of people had found the single adults group at a neighboring church supportive and helpful after their divorces.

After reviewing the various courses of action, individuals in crisis need to choose one or two upon which to embark. Gentle urging on the part of the minister may be required. I find it valuable to write down the commitment on a piece of paper for myself, and encourage counselees to write it down for themselves as well. They make a covenant to begin doing the chosen alternatives before the next visit, and thus embark on taking small, concrete steps toward achieving their goal.

Committing to Action. After the commitment, action must be immediate. This step is vital because it helps reverse any tendency toward ongoing dependence on the helper. Action counters the paralysis of crisis and encourages people to do something about their problems, whether they feel like it or not. O. Hobart Mowrer states, "It is easier to act your way into a new way of feeling than to feel your way into a new way of acting" (quoted in Clinebell 1966, 171). Or, in Clinebell's (n.d.) words, "The person's personality or self is like a muscle. When you use a muscle it grows stronger . . . if you don't use the muscle the muscle begins to atrophy and waste away." The resumption of personal control sometimes comes slowly but is accomplished over time.

Helpers need infinite patience. Sometimes people in crisis resist at this point; they "forget" or "don't have time" to begin acting on their chosen alternatives. They may be trying to make the helper angry in order to justify breaking off the helping relationship. The minister's task is to stay the course, go back two steps if need be, but continue the focus on "one small step that you can take today that will help you address your problem." Those who are being helped should not be allowed to slide by without at least recognizing their conduct. I repeatedly remind people of their freedom of choice to do or not to do that which will help them with their problems; I will help them to achieve their goals in any way I can but (except in extreme emergencies) will not achieve those goals for them.

Evaluating. In many ways, review and refinement are not a separate part of all helping, but an ongoing function. Ministers and those they help continually need to evaluate whether the chosen goals and new behaviors are effective toward resolution of the crisis. In the final sessions of crisis counseling it is always valuable to review the learning that has taken place, encouraging the use of newfound strengths and coping skills for the resolution of future problems and crises, which are certain to occur.

The task of crisis pastoral caregiving is to help persons in crisis regain at least their pre-crisis level of functioning, and possibly to grow to even higher levels. The model of crisis intervention that was offered here is an adaptation of the A-B-C method first formulated by Warren L. Jones and others. There are three basic elements of the A-B-C method of pastoral crisis intervention: (A) *A*chieve contact with the person; (B) *B*oil down the problem to its essentials; and (C) *C*ope actively with the problem. After a pastoral caregiver has used the A-B-C method of crisis intervention, it is important to follow up with those who have come through a crisis.

FOLLOW-UP

Follow-up with the person or family in crisis deepens the relationship and reaffirms the minister's concern. It determines whether or not they are continuing to do what is needed to resolve their crisis. It communicates that they have a continuing responsibility to do something specific about their problems. Following up does not mean checking up but showing interest in troubled persons' continued well-being. It also offers an additional chance for the expression of emotions and the assessing of the changes that are being made.

Follow-up also offers ministers a chance to deal with the fallout of a crisis event. Along with leftover feelings of hurt or anger, the gnawing anxiety that "it will happen again" sometimes persists. There may even be another, perhaps more basic, problem for which the person needs to seek counseling help. For example, while putting up a TV antenna on his house, a successful salesman fell from the roof and broke his back. The injury itself triggered a crisis for him and his wife, but as they discussed the problem with their minister it became apparent that they had serious marital problems as well. After resolving the initial crisis surrounding the injury, the couple began marriage counseling.

Follow-up can take place anywhere—over lunch in a café, in a phone call or a friendly stop at someone's workplace, a handwritten note, or a casual visit in the home. E-mail is less personal, but certainly can supplement other methods of follow-up as long as the helper remembers that e-mail messages are not confidential. All provide the occasion for ensuring a long-term resolution to the crisis.

RETURNING TO OUR CASE STUDY

Armed with a background of helpful crisis counseling methods from A to B to C, including follow-up, we return to the situation of Hector and Donna Martinez. Donna was firm about wanting a divorce and refused marriage counseling. It was evident to the pastor that Hector was under considerable stress. Using Switzer's three criteria for establishing the existence of a crisis, Pastor Cole found:

1. *A recent onset of bad feelings*: After six years of marriage, feelings had become overstrained on the previous Thursday night when Donna announced that she wanted a divorce.
2. *The feelings growing steadily worse*: They continued to intensify in Donna to the point where she forced Hector out of the house and started divorce proceedings, and they were so strong in Hector that he now was considering suicide.
3. *An external event triggering the recent surge of feeling*: There had been trouble in the marriage before, but it reached a new level of intensity with the Thursday-night fight when Donna told Hector that she was divorcing him.

Certain that this was a genuine crisis, Pastor Cole began to apply the A-B-C- method of crisis intervention.

Achieving Contact. Pastor Cole already had a relationship with Hector, having seen him in church regularly. The pastor was not rejecting or judgmental, even though Hector feared he might be. If Hector had not had a prior relationship of trust with Pastor Cole, he probably would not have sought counsel from anyone.

The pastor practiced most of the attending behaviors. He faced Hector, leaned toward him, and maintained eye contact. Hector responded to the attending behaviors and active listening, and in the second session broke down and sobbed. He said that since his wife left him he "didn't feel much of a man anymore." He felt he was totally without hope. He was cognitively constricted and could see no alternatives other than forcing Donna to live with him or committing suicide. The pastor allowed Hector to tell him the full story, and to lean upon and draw strength from him.

Boiling Down. Focusing the problem was somewhat difficult for the pastor in the second counseling session. Hector cried a great deal. He kept repeating: "If she doesn't come back I'm going to kill myself" and "I want my wife back—that's all I want." It was a long time before any two-way communication could develop. The pastor allowed considerable release of feelings but finally urged that they focus on what Hector could realistically do right away.

Another difficulty grew out of Pastor Cole's assumption that, because divorce was the precipitating event, it was the heart of the crisis. With continued listening, however, he was able to boil down the crisis to its central problem: "Hector, if I'm hearing you right, Donna's leaving you has left you feeling a deep loss and very lonely. You don't feel as much like a man as you used to." Hector responded, "Yeah, I feel like I've lost my manhood—it's terrible." In these brief summations, Hector and the pastor developed a *consensual formulation* of the essence of the crisis. They stated it as Hector most sharply experienced it. The crisis of Hector's loss and loneliness had caused within him a severe identity struggle. He relaxed somewhat (and so did Pastor Cole) after they felt they had articulated the crisis at its sharpest point. Sometimes just the process of developing a consensual formulation is all that is needed to turn around a crisis.

In this case, however, the pastor knew that he also had to challenge Hector to cope constructively through concrete action.

Before doing so, however, he needed to assess Hector's threats: "You are thinking of suicide? How do you plan on doing it? Do you own a gun? Do you have bullets? Is the gun loaded? Where is it?" (see chapter 4). Pastor Cole found that Hector did have a gun and ammunition with which to kill himself; the previous night he had even loaded the gun and played with it. He had decided *how* he would commit suicide, and he had the external *means* and the inner *stress* necessary to carry it out. This was a clear indication that Hector's suicide lethality was high and that the pastor would need to respond actively. Hector had to get rid of the gun—at least temporarily.

Coping Actively. Hector's only goal was to get his wife back. The pastor suggested that this goal did not appear likely, but that he would work with him on it and help him consider alternative ways of achieving it. The pastor inventoried Hector's resources with him, both internal and external, and concluded that he did not have many. He had not faced any severe crises in the past; he had few friends; he did not like his job and was afraid they might fire him if he continued complaining about his problems; he was a somewhat dependent person who had never developed much of an identity of his own. Pastor Cole summarized Hector's three main resources: his work (though he did not like this particular job, he did like the type of work he was doing); his brother and sister-in-law; and his pastor.

Because of Hector's limited resources, relatively high suicide lethality, and strong dependency, the pastor decided to end the second session by helping him write a calendar of all the things he would do in the three days before they next met: play chess during lunch with a friend at work, take his brother and sister-in-law out for a meal, return to a church school class he used to attend, and the like. He tried to ensure that Hector would be active and involved with people on each of those days. Hector agreed to live by that calendar. He further promised that he would call Pastor Cole at any time, day or night, if he felt he was going to commit suicide.

At the next session, Hector and the pastor discussed ways of reaching the goal of getting Donna to come back. Hector decided that because he had not been "much of a man," he would try to be more independent and autonomous rather than "acting like a baby like I am now." (It is important to remember, that the ownership of the goal is the counselees and they may not always choose the goal that we as pastoral caregivers would choose. It is essential that they choose the goal because then they are more likely to do it.) He chose several strategies to accomplish this goal and dedicated himself to them. He became more involved with people, made new friends, joined a community group, and acted more mature among his business associates in specific ways. The pastor challenged him whenever Hector appeared to become overly dependent on him or on others.

Hector chose several alternatives and he acted on them—not all in a week but within the space of three or four weeks. Whenever he came back to Pastor Cole saying he could not do a task he had committed to do, the pastor reflected, "It appears that you want to be led by the hand when we both know you can do it, and do it yourself." The pastor's response was slightly abrasive, but he felt that the relationship could tolerate it. Hector was angry, but he admitted that he could do it. He was just afraid. They talked about the fear, and role-played ways to handle an uncomfortable situation.

Soon after implementing his courses of action, Hector began to change his goal. As he worked through the initial weeks of grief, the former goal of "getting Donna back" evolved into the new goal of "being my own man"—being a more mature adult who, though deeply hurt by the loss of his marriage, wanted to become a better and more self-assured person.

After six sessions (about four weeks) Hector lost his job. Instead of crying over the layoff and threatening suicide, as he had done after his earlier loss, he made up résumés and flew to a trade convention in Chicago where he received several job offers. This experience was gratifying and helped him to continue acting more as a competent adult.

After the crisis was resolved, the pastor referred Hector to a self-help group in the church. In the company of other growing persons he continued to develop his skills for healthy interpersonal relationships—and an identity of his own. In his own words, "I am becoming more of a man."

REFERRAL

"Properly conceived, referral is a means of using a team effort to help a troubled person. . . . It employs the division-of-labor principle that is the basis of interprofessional cooperation" (Clinebell 1984, 311). There are two types of referral. In one, the helper gives the major responsibility for care over to another professional. This type is frequently necessary when a person in crisis is psychotic, suicidal or homicidal, or needs hospitalization. The other form of referral, more common to the minister doing crisis counseling, involves retaining major responsibility for the care but sending troubled individuals to specialists or self-help groups for specific types of help (for example, to a family debt counselor for assistance with financial planning).

Referral to outside professionals or self-help groups is not a sign of failure. Often it is inevitable. Even if one is a good pastoral carer, a healer, a guide, a reconciler, and a sustainer, it is nevertheless the mark of an effective crisis intervener to know when and how to refer. Referral is a matter of timing, taking into consideration both the state of the person in crisis and the helper's own limitations. Time, skill, and emotional objectivity all play a role in determining when it is best to send a person to more specialized care.

Time

Assuming the pastoral carer has the expertise to deal with a particular person's crisis, it is important to determine whether she or he has the time to handle the situation adequately (and often immediately). One should answer quite frankly: Will I seriously neglect my other responsibilities because of the time given to these individuals? Can I really limit them to only so many minutes or so many sessions per week? Can I honestly and firmly restrict telephone availability? Will such limitations involve a cost to the healing process?

Skill

Even when time is sufficient, in some crisis situations one helper's distinctive complex of skills and experience will be far less helpful to the individual than that of a counselor or caregiver or self-help group which has some highly developed facility for dealing with a particular problem. A good illustration is heroin addiction; unless actively working with a drug treatment center, few caregivers are equipped to treat it effectively.

Some questions to ask in determining if a helper has the necessary skills to handle a particular crisis include: Do I feel comfortable working with this person? Can I be sure I am not misinterpreting this person's situation? After perhaps three or four sessions, is the person showing change? Am I fostering negative dependency?

As a rule of thumb, it is important to consider referring to a mental health professional any person who is or appears to be psychotic, violent, seriously suicidal, homicidal, or whose behavior is noticeably bizarre.

Emotional Objectivity

Even if one has sufficient time and skills that are adequate to a particular problem, it is important to examine one's own emotional objectivity. Because of personal beliefs or values or one's own past difficulties in resolving similar problems, some situations may elicit within the helper feelings of insecurity or hostility, threat or fear. Is this problem one that I have faced but never successfully resolved? Am I so overburdened emotionally because of work and family commitments that I have little left to offer this individual? Do I find myself needing the other's approval so that it is difficult to intervene with integrity and authority? Or am I becoming overly involved emotionally with the person or the situation? If the answer to any of these is yes, it is time to refer.

In every phase of the care process, whether in establishing a relationship, working out a course of action, or referring to another, the pastoral carer's effective functioning depends upon the degree to which she or he understands all the limitations of the situation and acts creatively out of a sense of emotional security, stability, and relative objectivity. When referral is required, the following ideas may apply:

- Keep in mind that not everyone will accept suggestions for referral. Some may only want to complain about a situation and not work toward a solution. For others, just talking about the problem and considering a referral is sufficient motivation to action.

- Make referrals in a tactful, concrete way: not, "I think you should see a shrink," but "I'd be happy to recommend several marriage counselors—Dr. Gomez was especially helpful with my sister and I've heard very good things about Dr. Utt from several people who have seen her."

- When uncertain of where to refer, call a mental health professional in the congregation, a local crisis line, or an information and referral agency. Explain the situation, and obtain up-to-date information on the person or agency to which one is referring. Sometimes calling the office directly can be helpful in learning whether a waiting list exists, how long it might be, the fee schedule, and any other pertinent information.

- Suggest several referral sources if possible, because one professional may not be available immediately.

- Do not (except in an emergency) make the referral call on behalf of the person in crisis. The individual needs to initiate the call. But it may be helpful to suggest dialing the number immediately or to offer a ride (if you are willing to offer this) to the first appointment.

- Remember that referral is not the first step in the care process, except in an emergency. Establish a relationship, listen carefully to the person's pain, and then gently begin to nudge toward doing something about the problem, noting how the suggested referral source can benefit the person in the resolution of the crisis.

- After referring, follow up. Call the next day to express in a nonjudgmental way, "I called to see how you are today, and to find out if there were any problems in scheduling a session with Dr. Gomez or Dr. Utt." If the person gives excuses, ask if there are any further ways to help or if the individual would like to discuss any other things with you. Mention that you will call back in a couple of days to see how things are going. Be as sensitive as possible neither to hound anyone nor to let him or her shrug off the needed care easily.

The A-B-C method of crisis intervention allows helpers to respond to people in a wide range of situational crises. The *A* of the A-B-C method invites the minister to achieve contact—to establish a relationship with the troubled person. The *B* is boiling down the problem to its essentials; it covers responding and focusing the pastoral conversation on the specifics of the crisis. The *C* calls for the person in crisis to cope actively with the difficulty. It includes a five-part problem management method that helps break crisis paralysis and moves individuals into action. Together these three tasks provide a way that clergy and lay pastoral caregivers can respond to those in crisis, offering support in their isolation, clarity in their confusion, and direction and hope as they take steps toward a new future.

4

EXTREME INTERVENTIONS

For most clergy, crises are a normal part of the workweek. People in their care experience bereavement, job loss, discovery of a spouse's infidelity, teenage pregnancy, cancer, abandonment, divorce—and they are thrown into turmoil. At such times they often turn to the pastor for support.

But occasionally ministers are drawn into situations that are not so common, that are tougher, more complex, and even more dangerous than those human crises they face with regularity.

Hurricane Katrina devastates the southern part of Louisiana and Mississippi and surrounding areas; there is a shooting in the local high school; a tornado sweeps through Oklahoma City, laying waste a mobile home park and a large section of a residential neighborhood; a 747 collides with a small private plane and everyone aboard both planes dies; a terrorist attack kills thousands in New York City; a school bus hits a patch of ice and skids off an overpass, killing many children, including a number of siblings. These are not just big news stories. They don't always happen somewhere else. Every day, pastors and church members are called upon to respond to situations that affect a large number of people in the community, state, nation, or world.

Extreme emergencies are not always global. The pastor's phone rings at 2 A.M. and the minister stumbles for the receiver. An unfamiliar voice blurts: "You don't know me, but I just wanted to tell someone why I'm doing this. I can't take it anymore. I can't keep living this way. I have fifty Secanols and I've already taken half of them . . ."

The pastor of a small-town church gets a call from a deputy who tells him that the sheriff is out of town and the postmaster, a solitary but apparently respectable man, ". . . has gone berserk! He has a gun and he's taken two hostages and he's making all kinds of crazy demands. I know he went to your church once in a while—can you come and talk to him?"

The church's secretary and its female pastor are besieged with a series of obscene and subtly threatening telephone calls by an individual who is often incoherent and expresses a deep hatred of women.

A woman runs into a minister's office in a panic—her daughter and son-in-law (who live next door to the church) have been arguing for three days, and it has suddenly escalated into a violent physical fight. "Would you please do something to stop them before someone gets hurt?"

The A-B-C method of crisis intervention facilitates intervention for most problems that a pastor may encounter. But extreme circumstances such as those mentioned above, however rare, cause great concern to those trying to offer care. Threatened homicide or suicide, physical abuse, kidnapping or the taking of a hostage, a grisly death, an explosion at a plant, or a commercial airline disaster are crisis situations that may call for additional and distinctive modes of intervention.

This chapter touches on such crucial interventions. It covers telephone emergencies, suicide threats, high-risk situations, and threats to the helper's safety.

TELEPHONE CRISIS INTERVENTION

Most telephone conversation is casual and light. It is like dinner-table talk; topic after topic comes up and the quality of listening is not always as important as the spirit of telling stories of the day's events. Consequently, it is sometimes difficult for crisis interveners to make the transition from conversational telephone discourse to crisis counseling over the telephone. Even in a dire emergency, habitual ways of responding on the phone may creep into telephone conversation if pastoral caregivers are not careful. The relationship with a caller in crisis is neither social nor antisocial; it must be a working pastoral relationship.

Over-the-Phone Crisis Counseling

Face-to-face crisis intervention benefits from nonverbal signals that fill in the meaning behind the words. How people position themselves in a chair and gesticulate while talking, their overall demeanor, and especially their facial gestures and eye contact (or lack thereof) aid a helper's understanding of what they are saying. In telephone intervention all these visual data are missing, so helpers need to listen carefully for other nonverbal cues such as voice tonality, pauses, tension or tightness of the throat, crying or choked sobs. In addition, because callers cannot get visual or non-verbal cues, helpers must add their own verbal cues in order for callers to realize that they are listening and responding.

Williams and Douds, social workers at a suicide prevention center, note four features of crisis intervention work over the telephone (Lester 2002, 58–63). The first is *control*. In face-to-face conversation, the troubled person usually has to come to the office, wait for the pastor, and learn the amount of time available for the session; therefore, the pastor has greater influence than over the phone. In telephone crisis intervention the troubled individual initiates the contact with the helper and may terminate it at any moment. If the helper says anything that the caller perceives as challenging or offensive, the caller can hang up.

A second characteristic of telephone counseling is that it allows *anonymity*. For some this anonymity gives greater freedom to say what is on their minds; they are more open to conveying over the phone what they might not reveal in a face-to-face encounter. Although caller ID makes phone conversations less anonymous than they once were, most people in crisis are still concerned about their privacy.

The third characteristic of crisis phone work is that frequently the *helper is not known* by the caller. This promotes positive trans-ference; the callers' fantasies of what they want in a caring individual sometimes can be better realized over the phone than in person.

Accessibility is the fourth feature of telephone crisis inter-vention work. Most individuals have telephones and are able to contact a helper whenever they wish. Cell phones make this even more possible. Accessibility is vital in crises, many of which occur outside typical office hours. For example, a great many individuals who threaten suicide do so in the middle of the night. The tele-phone call may be the only contact they can achieve with someone who will help them make it through the night.

Difficult Calls

Most crisis helpers eventually discover that, for whatever reason, some people who use the phone claim an emergency when none exists. As a working hypothesis, however, the helper must accept what they are told at face value. The truth sometimes is stranger than any bogus situation a caller can invent.

The first task when one receives a telephone call of distress is to find out the person's name, phone number, and address, if possible. This responsibility is so obvious that it is sometimes overlooked. Caller ID can help, and all ministers would do well to have this feature on every telephone that can receive calls from the public. A crisis call may inadvertently disconnect; if the helper does not know the caller's name or telephone number, it is impossible to follow up. Some years ago a very distraught man threatening suicide called me from a pay phone. While talking he accidentally touched the phone cradle and was cut off. I called him back immediately. He had used his last coin to make that call and was so upset by one more thing going wrong that, he told me, "I figured what's the use, I might as well end it." Most people will give their name and number as an automatic response if asked in a matter-of-fact way, early in the conversation. If they refuse, it is best not to force the issue but to continue the conversation and ask again at a later stage.

After getting the name and phone number of the caller, it is important to determine the parameters of the problem—Does the crisis involve other persons, and if so, how many? Where are these other persons? Are drugs or alcohol involved? Are weapons on the premises or have any weapons been used? Has there been any abuse or any injuries or threat of injuries? If there have been injuries, how serious are they?—and so forth.

Some calls, by their very nature, are more difficult and require additional knowledge and preparation. Repeated calls, prank calls, and sexual calls are demanding and require special attention. The following paragraphs examine these types of calls.

Repeat Calls. Repeat calls occasionally come in from individuals who have such poor personal resources or lack of insight that they continually find themselves in crisis situations. However, the majority of repeat callers know what they need to do but put off making decisions and taking action. They talk on the phone as a way to avoid participating in serious counseling or therapy. (In my experience some of these individuals also repeatedly call the church secretary or make frequent visits to the church office.)

It is important to determine whether chronic callers are genuinely asking for help or are in some way avoiding taking responsibility for their problems. Those who lack resources or insight need as much care as the caregiver has time to offer. (The helper who does not have the time or energy to deal with such calls should refer them to someone else.) Those who know what they need to do but refuse to take action require a different response. Ministers should be aware that some repeat callers may contact a number of people in the church; if they do not get the desired response from one person, they go on to the next. Therefore, ministers or leaders of lay pastoral-care groups need to keep all helpers alert to these multiple contacts by chronic callers, determine a planned response to them, and inform all helpers of the plan.

With either type of chronic caller, it is imperative to determine if a real emergency exists. The first type of caller is likely to have a number of real emergencies that call for typical crisis intervention methods. The second type of chronic caller does not usually have a real crisis but merely wishes to complain or to vent anger. In any case, you need to be sure.

Prank Calls. The second class of difficult phone calls is prank calls. Some people call a caregiver, pretend they have a problem, and describe it in all its gory detail. After a few minutes, bad acting skills or factual inconsistencies usually make it obvious that this is a prank call and it is time for the helper to put an end to the conversation.

The more difficult prank call is silent. The helper answers the telephone, and no one responds at the other end of the line. The problem with silence is that some individuals in crisis are so overwrought that they have trouble putting their pain into words. Without the benefit of visual cues, one cannot determine whether the quiet on the other end of the line is a trick or the silence of a person struggling for courage and/or words to express deep distress.

When a caller is silent, it is best to remain calm and make statements such as "It's hard to talk about your problems (to someone you don't know)" or "Sometimes it's hard to put into words what you are feeling." Allow for longish pauses. After three or four minutes of silence it is usually wise to tell silent callers that when they get to a place where they are able to talk, they should feel welcome to call back. Then hang up.

Sexual Calls

Most sexual callers do not want help; they attempt to involve the crisis intervener in their sexual activities. Some call a crisis helper of the opposite (or same) sex and masturbate while telling some story or another. They may do little more than breathe, repeating phrases such as "Talk to me," "Don't leave me," or "Let me finish." Take a direct approach to these callers. Tell them that if they have a problem to discuss, you are willing to talk with them in the future. Then terminate the call.

Obscene telephone calls, another type of sexual call, are familiar to most ministers and crisis hotline volunteers. Again the helper does best to tell such callers that if they want to talk about their problems on another occasion they may do so, and then hang up.

In a third type of sexual call, the caller tries to get the helper into a conversation about sex. Such conversations may begin with indirect comments but become increasingly more explicit in his or her descriptions of sexual activities. These callers may masturbate while recounting their sexual fantasies. One of the simplest ways of differentiating a true sexual problem from a bogus one is to listen for hesitancy or embarrassment on the part of the caller. Most people experience some difficulty talking about sexual problems if they are real. They will stammer or speak haltingly while trying to relate their troubles. Callers who are using the phone to share their sexual fantasies are bolder, and many times will abruptly end the conversation themselves before the crisis intervener has a chance to discontinue it.

SUICIDE

Whether on the telephone or in a face-to-face conference, one of the most alarming situations a helper will encounter is a person who is or may be suicidal. At such times it is essential to listen for the seriousness of suicide risk—in other words, to make judgments about the lethality of the suicide threat. The assessment of suicide lethality is an additional task of the B—boiling down and focusing—of the A-B-C method of crisis counseling discussed in the previous chapter. The following series of factors can help one *gauge the seriousness of suicide threats* (Farberow, Heilig, and Litman 1968; Stone 1991).

The helper should not use these nine basic criteria as a routine checklist but internalize them, obtaining the answers informally but directly in conversation with the potentially suicidal person. These nine factors give caregivers a way to judge the seriousness of the talk of suicide. Although all talk of suicide must be taken seriously, on some occasions caregivers will gauge the potential for suicide high and must call 911 to get immediate help for the person. On other occasions, it will become clear to the caregiver that there is little immediate threat and a less aggressive approach is appropriate. So read over these nine basic criteria and use them to make a judgment concerning someone's suicide lethality. Do seek help from another minister, mental health worker, or the local crisis hotline as you consider these criteria regarding a potentially suicidal individual.

Age and Gender

A person's age and gender is a statistical factor in suicide. Although women more often attempt it, over half (55 percent) of completed suicides are men. The threat of suicide increases in lethality with age, especially among men. Therefore, if both a seventeen-year-old girl and a man in his seventies are threatening suicide, and all other factors are roughly equal, the man is statistically more likely to complete the act. Never forget, however, that all talk of suicide is serious. Suicide among teenagers has risen dramatically in the last thirty years even though it remains statistically lower than for older adults.

Suicide Plan

Is suicide a vague, general threat, or does the person have a specific plan for how to go about it? This is the most critical element in assessing suicide risk. The pastoral carer will have to determine how *specific* the plan is, how *lethal* the method, and how *available* the means for putting the plan into effect. The answers to these questions generally will not be available through just listening, but will require direct and forthright questioning of the troubled person. Some methods of committing suicide are obviously more lethal than others: a gun is more dangerous than tranquilizers, a full bottle of barbiturates more deadly than a handful of aspirin. If a person has a very specific plan, has spent time thinking in detail about how to commit the act, has selected a lethal method, and has the means readily available, *the risk of suicide is very serious and requires immediate action* on the part of the intervener.

Crisis

People in a crisis triggered by a loss or impending loss, such as death, divorce, or illness, account for many serious threats of suicide. A number of people in crisis will consider suicide as one possible way of coping with the adversity. If there is *extreme distress* and the individual has a *specific suicide plan*, then the helper must respond even more actively.

Symptoms

Suicide can result from several different emotional states, among them depression, psychosis, and agitation. The most serious is the depressed-agitated state, in which a person feels emotionally depressed but simultaneously tense and active, and therefore possesses the necessary energy and determination to complete the act. Contrary to popular myth, however, not everyone who commits suicide is depressed.

Other categories of individuals at risk for suicide are the recently bereaved or divorced, gay males, individuals who have attempted suicide before, alcoholics and other substance abusers, people recently diagnosed with a terminal illness, and sexual deviants. Each of these groups has a relatively high suicide rate.

Meaning and Religious Involvement

People who are neither influenced by nor committed to any religious group or belief system generally feel freer to complete the act of suicide. Strong religious beliefs and regular involvement with some church or religious group provide both emotional support and social constraint against suicide. Nevertheless, even deeply religious people sometimes take their own lives.

Resources

Although people who are suicidal may feel they have no resources, the pastoral caregiver knows that usually they have more resources than they realize. It is essential to identify relatives, friends, church members, social workers, coworkers, and others who are available to assist suicidal individuals through their crisis. Above all, encourage them to be frank with others about the seriousness of their difficulties. In the case of one who appears suicidal and seems immobilized, it may be a good idea to inform some of their resource persons of the suicide potential so they can become involved and actively communicate their caring. When people who are considering suicide have (or perceive they have) few personal resources, then the pastor and lay pastoral caregivers—as the representative presence of the church—can reach out to them, broadening their network of resources and providing support as they grapple with their predicament.

Lifestyle

A relatively stable lifestyle—perceivable by indicators like consistent work history, long marriage and enduring family relations, and absence of past suicide attempts—provides some measure of deterrence from suicide. Unstable individuals may exhibit chronic addiction, job hopping or marriage hopping, character disorder or psychosis, frequent unresolved crises, and so on. Chronic suicide threats happen only among unstable personalities, but acute suicidal gestures may occur among people with either stable or unstable lifestyles.

Communication

The individual who has stopped communicating with others may have given up hope and is more likely to attempt suicide. Indirect, nonverbal communication that one is having thoughts of ending life (making a new will, giving up prized possessions or favorite activities, and so forth) is as important as direct verbal threat; unfortunately, indirect communication seldom reaches ministers and other helping professionals. Family and friends may be the only ones to notice such signs of distress, and they can provide the pastor or mental health professional with vital information regarding the lethality of the threat. Sometimes, tragically, no one notices. By maintaining contact with key laypersons, pastors may hear of people whose behavior indicates they are at risk, and then seek them out before they act on their suicide impulses.

Medical Fears

The helper should determine if a suicidal individual has (or fears) a serious disease, such as cancer, AIDS, a chronic illness, or an impending or recent surgery. Individuals with a terminal illness may be attracted to suicide as a way of coping with or avoiding pain. Some people have committed suicide believing they had cancer when in fact they did not.

With the exception of a specific and lethal plan, none of the above criteria is necessarily dangerous when taken alone. It is important to gather all the information and look at the whole picture to see if a pattern is beginning to form.

Take all ideas about suicide seriously. This is the basic underlying rule in dealing with suicide, even the hint of it. When a person says, "I'm tired of trying," "Life isn't worth living anymore," "There is no way out," or the like, the minister should ask directly if she or he is contemplating suicide. It simply is not true that talking about suicide will encourage a person to do it; talking about it in frank and specific detail (so that one can offer assistance) is much better than ignoring it. Whenever there is even the slightest chance of such a possibility, the assessment of suicide lethality is a necessary addition to the B (boiling down) phase of crisis counseling.

HIGH-RISK CRISIS SITUATIONS

There are certain occasions when helpers find themselves offering care in extremely difficult situations: people who are suicidal, enraged, mentally disturbed, or potentially violent; domestic disputes; kidnapping or hostage taking, and the like. All involve extra risk, and all call for extra measures. Ministers will want to opt out of some of these situations—and should opt out, if they can pass to a more appropriate intervener—but it is possible to find oneself in the middle of a high-risk situation and have no choice but to act. It has happened to me on several occasions and I suspect it has happened to many pastors.

In such cases, helpers' first concern must be for their own personal safety (discussed in detail at the end of this chapter). This is no time for heroics. If possible, one should get assistance and work as part of a team. Sharing the burden with other helpers allows time to think about responses, avoid overreacting, and benefit from other perspectives. Collaborative efforts in high-risk crises are best for both the helper and the person in crisis. (In fact, many communities have crisis or disaster response teams that include clergy among the first responders.)

Developing Relationships

The following suggestions focus on structuring relationships and negotiating decisions in demanding or volatile circumstances. Some approaches work best for developing relationships with people who have probably had poor interpersonal relationships in the past.

Establishing rapport with people who are threatening suicide or who are violent requires more finesse on the part of crisis interveners. They must be able to develop relationships with a wide range of individuals: corporate lawyers as well as revivalists hawking tracts on corners, homeless people and those who live in elegant and expensive homes, counterculturists and middle-class retirees, prisoners and computer programmers, prostitutes and teachers, gardeners, entertainers, machinists—an endless variety of human beings. Helpers sometimes have a very narrow range of people to whom they can effectively offer care—mostly people like themselves: middle class, educated, religious, emotionally sensitive, and motivated. Helpers who are uncomfortable with people who are very different from themselves need to uncover their limitations, stretch out, develop a capacity for relating to a wider spectrum of human experience.

How ministers go about establishing a relationship with people in crisis is particularly important in high-risk situations. Interveners must exercise great flexibility in the way they position themselves in relation to persons in distress. They must listen carefully for clues that will tell them how the troubled ones want to define the relationship. (For example, potentially violent individuals with a background in crime, though acting aggressively, may still see themselves as having little worth. Thus, they may distrust helpers who treat them with deference; they may be more comfortable with the helper who takes a slightly superior posture in the relationship.) The most common mistake is to act as if the person in crisis is a close friend. Sometimes helpers who feel uncomfortable or frightened may act overly friendly, not realizing that the troubled person may find such warmth and kindliness foreign and treat it with suspicion.

Using the Right Words

One of the first tasks in establishing a relationship in difficult situations is to determine how to address troubled persons. What do they want to be called? The pastoral caregiver can simply ask, "What is your name?" or "What shall I call you?" (It is best not to address individuals by their first names unless they request it; uninvited familiarity may suggest an insincere chumminess and lead to mistrust.) If they do not give a name, refer to them as "you." After the conversation has progressed, say, "I'm a little uncomfortable just saying 'you.' Would you be willing to tell me your name or a name I may use?"

While most crisis situations may allow the intervener some margin for error in address, in highly volatile circumstances a small detail like the helper's word choices can make or break the relationship. Phrases that can block effectiveness include the royal "we," as in: "We all get angry at our children." Many individuals find "we" to be condescending, particularly if they interpret it as meaning "you." It is also good to avoid absolutes—terms like "always," "any," "all," or "never."

Another less-than-helpful response from crisis interveners is the phrase, "That is all I am asking of you." It sounds patronizing. It may prompt a negative reaction. "Would you mind . . ." or another tentatively stated request also might backfire. For example, a person threatening suicide calls and indicates she has barbiturates; if you respond by saying "Would you mind bringing the pills to my office?" she may well think (or even say), "Yes, I would mind."

Perhaps due to poor childhood relationships with their parents, many individuals in high-risk circumstances are hypersensitive to anything they perceive as condescending or demeaning. Therefore, pastoral caregivers must take care to avoid expressing themselves in parental ways, neither scolding nor cheering up (which only serves to discount the pain and suffering of the depressed or distressed).

Finally, helpers need to be careful not to use religious or psychological buzzwords. Anxious individuals may not understand your jargon, and it may cause them to become even more confused, upset, or enraged.

Defusing Volatile Situations

The good news for pastoral carers who are anxious about dealing with a dangerous crisis is that certain methods effectively defuse emotions and restore stability in high-risk circumstances. One such technique that is sometimes useful in discussing alternative courses of action with people who are greatly upset and agitated is called the "illusion of alternatives" (Everstine and Everstine 2006). Most parents have used this ploy with their children: "Which vegetable would you prefer for supper: peas, or broccoli?" The children appear to have a choice (peas, broccoli) but the parents determine the alternatives; they do not offer the choice of not eating vegetables. Likewise, when an agitated or suicidal individual needs to go to the hospital for review and possible confinement, the illusion of alternatives may serve well: "Would you like me to arrange for the police to take you or would you rather have a family member drive you there?" The helper, having determined (with appropriate consultation) that such an evaluation is essential, does not offer the choice of going or not going to the hospital. Most people who are given transportation options will choose one of them—usually a relative—to deliver them to the hospital. This method is not without danger, but intervention in very demanding situations sometimes requires risky methods.

Another useful method in difficult situations is acting slightly confused when responding to a highly upset individual. I will sometimes say, "I want to make certain that I understand you correctly," and then repeat back what I heard in a slightly inaccurate way. Most people want to make certain they are understood properly; oftentimes they will rechannel their energy from explosive outbursts to explanations and corrections.

A similar procedure is *reframing* (Stone 1994). There are several different reframing interventions; in one, the minister defuses a potentially explosive situation by placing a more favorable frame or connotation onto the actions of one or more of the combatants. For example, if a woman has accused her husband of being a workaholic who is "never home, doesn't care to spend time with the family, is only interested in his career," I may suggest that his attention to his work reveals that he is very concerned about his family's comfort and financial well-being, and is a good provider. This is not a Pollyanna response nor is it the power of positive thinking. It is a restructuring of the situation to highlight positives that are truly present in what the troubled persons have said or done.

Oddly enough, *humor* is another useful approach to high-risk situations. It has a way of disarming people in crisis, diverting their attention from what is upsetting them. I am not suggesting that the caregiver make light of a person's difficulty. If you can find the humor in a situation without demeaning or embarrassing any of the people involved, a little laughter may help to break the tension.

It is important to note, in general, that therapeutic maneuvers or counseling methods which are useful for office encounters may be inappropriate in people's homes. When helpers leave their offices they give up some of their professional persona and authority, and they need to act more tentatively. Consequently, some of the confrontive or assertive interventions that could be accomplished easily in the pastor's office are not carried out as easily in a parishioner's living room.

Discerning Perceptions of the Helpers

Most helpers are good, positive, well-meaning people—solid members of the church and community. They consider themselves to be nonthreatening, caring individuals, genuinely interested in giving comfort to those in need. But people who threaten harm to others or vow to take their own lives may not see the helper in the same light. They may have spent most of their lives reacting to people who tell them what to do; they may have little or no experience with one who is genuinely interested in them. Do not assume that a troubled person will perceive you as the compassionate, helpful, earnest person that you are.

Quick Action Requires Careful Thought

Immediate action is essential in crisis intervention work. But when helpers respond to the dangerously crucial situations described in this chapter, helpers must give themselves time to think about what to say and how to respond.

Know how you typically respond in tense or crisis situations. Do you talk too little or too much? Many helpers compensate for their own anxiety by asking too many questions. This may be counterproductive because many distressed people have spent much of their lives answering the questions of people in authority, and they do not like it. When I face a tricky circumstance my natural tendency is to move at a faster pace, to talk and act more quickly. I have to slow down my anxiety-driven reactions. I must give myself time to think before I act. Lives may depend upon it.

PERSONAL SAFETY

In most congregations, clergy work among a milder sort of humanity. Most of their parishioners are not accustomed to being beaten or slapped around, nor do they daily interact with people under the influence of alcohol and other drugs. As a result, caregivers may fail to take the necessary personal safety precautions when responding to crises. In 99 percent of the situations ministers encounter, this naïveté will create no problem. In a small fraction of instances, however, crisis interveners must act with caution. Frightened or angry people who feel trapped may act in ways that are utterly foreign to most helpers' experience.

Over the years I have come to believe more and more that safety is an important element of crisis counseling. Perhaps it is my age; perhaps it is the memory of being in dangerous circumstances on several occasions. Or it may be my knowledge of several ministers who were threatened (in two cases, injured) that has caused me to pay more attention to personal protection. The following considerations need to become elements of intervention in crises, especially in hazardous or volatile contexts.

First, if at all possible, *do not go to the scene of an emergency situation*; it is much better to arrange for a neutral site or office visit. When telephone calls come at night it is usually better to talk people through a situation on the phone than to go to the scene. Arranging for a family member or friend to stay through the night with an individual who is suicidal and making an appointment for the following morning is often sufficient. In addition, one good approach is to develop a suicide contract with such persons in which they pledge not to do anything to harm themselves between the time of the call and the next morning's session.

There are times, day or night, when helpers must go to the scene of a serious crisis. The following suggestions address such occasions.

Do not go to the site alone, ever, especially at night. Police officers usually ask for backup when called to critical situations. They know, for example, that each year more police officers are injured responding to domestic disputes than in any other circumstance. If the possibility of harm exists, ministers should simply not go, at least not without assistance. At such times, when it is tempting to think of others' needs, you must focus on the needs of your own family.

Beforehand, it is good for ministers to have chosen particular individuals who can respond to a call for assistance at a moment's notice. Members of self-help groups such as Alcoholics Anonymous are especially valuable; they are used to getting up in the middle of the night to help others in difficulty. Do not hesitate to call on the police for assistance; in fact, if a weapon or physical violence is involved, their presence is vital. It has been my experience that police will seldom give a minister a hard time for overreacting. One officer responded to my apologies by saying, "I'd rather have you err in the direction of calling me when there is no danger than to err by not calling me when there is danger. Then I have two problems. I have to separate the disputants *and* I have to try to protect you from danger."

When driving to the scene, park several houses away so that you can make a slow, cautious approach to the house, listening for sounds and keeping an eye out for any disturbances. Move cautiously to the door and listen some more. After knocking, stand back and off to the side of the door in case anyone comes bursting through it. When someone answers the door, introduce yourself, but do not enter the house unless invited. If the person at the door asks you in but someone inside tells you to leave, either stay outside or leave the scene. By now, the situation described on the phone may have radically changed. The caller expressed only one view of the situation; others may be displeased or angry about the call and do not want you involved.

If you must enter a strange room, move slowly. Scan it, looking for signs of violence: broken furniture, glass, or evidence that people have been fighting. Look also for weapons. If the room is dark, enter with even greater caution, and ask for permission to turn on a light. Once inside, attempt to keep all disputants in front of you and in view. Don't let anyone get behind you. Urge family members to sit down and stay in the room, unless you are separating the disputants and sending one of them to another room with another helper.

Try to be the one who chooses where conversations will take place. Even though the kitchen is a comfortable place where people can sit over a cup of coffee and talk informally, it is not a good place to be in dangerous situations because it holds too many potential weapons. The bedroom is another bad idea because most people store their firearms there. The dining room or living room is a safer site for conversation in potentially violent crises.

Strive to gain control of the emergency situation in any way possible without becoming physically involved. One of the first tasks is to get everyone seated, because there is less danger when people are less mobile. Be sure to sit down with the others; to remain standing while others are seated may be the body language of a negative authority figure. Choose a hard-backed chair; it is not likely to be someone's favorite chair. It is a good idea to sit near an outside door so that if hostilities flare again, a quick exit is possible.

Do not feign heroism. If the situation appears to be beyond your abilities, or if you become concerned about your own or another's safety, leave immediately. Get help. Once again, it never hurts to call the police for assistance if the crisis is beyond your control. In many communities helpers can inform the police of the visit beforehand and ask them to wait nearby; in any case it is good to have an existing relationship with the local police in order to avoid needing to explain who you are in the heat of a crisis.

Finally, however skilled at establishing relationships, however prepared with techniques of high-risk intervention, and however cautious in dangerous circumstances, sometimes the best pastoral caregivers direct people in crisis to professionals who specialize in the particular types of care that will best meet their needs. This point applies especially to difficult or dangerous situations; in cases such as this chapter describes, referral often is essential.

Chapter 3 provided a detailed description of referral. The pastoral carer who is unsure about the best course in one of these tough crises, or who recognizes the need for some specific outside skill or resource, must view referral not as an admission of incompetence—because it is not—but as the act of a skilled professional. It may be the sane and unheroic deed that saves a human life.

5

PORTRAITS IN CRISIS

Not all crises were created the same. That seems obvious but none-theless deserves mention, because in developing methods for man-aging crises one may be tempted to overlook the uniqueness of each individual human situation. An obvious danger is that what worked to resolve one crisis may fail in the next. But crises have common themes and experiences, and they do form clusters that share sufficient characteristics to make their study fruitful.

Caplan, Mason, and Kaplan (1965, 151), researchers in the field of crisis theory, believe that crises differ in two ways: accord-ing to whether they are developmental or situational; and accord-ing to the type of challenge or hazard involved, such as death of a loved one or a significant personal injury. They found that, despite a diversity of precipitators, within any cluster of crisis types some psychological tasks appear to occur regularly and repeatedly. The precipitators of crises can be as varied as the people who experi-ence them, yet there are some basic dynamics at the core of every crisis. Were this not the case, we would not be able to study crisis intervention in general, but only the dynamics and treatment of specific cases.

To demonstrate the applicability of generalized crisis theory to a multiplicity of situations, this chapter describes several dif-ferent cases of people in crisis, and shows how the A-B-C method of crisis intervention was used in each case. I suggest that readers project themselves into the situation and not only think about how to counsel the person in each case—there is no one best way—but also try to define the precipitator of the crisis, the individual's per-ception of it, and, with the details presented, a consensual formu-lation for the person.

A CASE OF ALZHEIMER'S DISEASE

Dorothy and Clint Jacobson were lifelong members of a Lutheran church in a small northwestern Wisconsin town. Dorothy had retired early from her teaching career to take care of her husband.

Their pastor, Janice Rue, knew that Clint had been diagnosed as having Alzheimer's disease. Pastor Rue visited the Jacobsons regularly and offered her help or that of the congregation, but Dorothy always refused. She was obviously embarrassed about her husband's condition. The Jacobsons belonged to the school of thought that "a family takes care of its own."

Immediate Situation

Dorothy went to a neighbor's house to borrow several eggs for some baking, got into a conversation, and was delayed ten or fifteen minutes. When she returned home, her husband was gone. Dorothy was not concerned at first; he would sometimes wander out to the garage and tinker. But this time he was not there. After checking with neighbors and still not locating him, she became worried that he had walked into the nearby woods, and she called the police. She also called Pastor Rue.

Intervention

The police, members of the church, and people in the community searched for Clint Jacobson all afternoon and evening to no avail. Pastor Rue alternated spending time with Dorothy, searching in the woods, and calling members of her congregation and several neighboring ones for additional help.

Clint Jacobson was found early the next morning—cold, dehydrated, and hungry—over eight miles from his house. Everyone breathed a sigh of relief. He was hospitalized for observation and released in good health the next day.

Dorothy was at her wit's end after Clint came home from the hospital. Everyone was excited and congratulated her (and themselves) for finding him, but she now knew she had a sizable problem on her hands. She could never again leave Clint alone.

The months and perhaps years of taking care of Clint twenty-four hours a day, as he would increasingly lose mental facilities and even urinary control, stretched out before Dorothy. Their two daughters lived in distant cities. Dorothy was not in the habit of asking for help. But she also was not able to handle the strain of caring for her husband day in, day out.

Janice Rue realized that Dorothy was crumbling under the strain of caring for her husband. Clint's walk in the woods was the last straw; Dorothy's fear of losing him had paralyzed her. She could hardly prepare a meal for herself or her husband, and had slept little in three days when Janice Rue finally intervened. Alone with Pastor Rue, Dorothy began to shake physically and had difficulty stopping.

Janice Rue sat with Dorothy and told her that she obviously had to make changes. Dorothy agreed that things could not go on as they had been. She also agreed that she could no longer hide Clint's illness from the neighbors.

Over the next four or five days, Pastor Rue worked as an advocate, a strong voice for change, and a compassionate listener. She sat down with Dorothy and her daughters, who had flown in during the crisis, and as a group they made some decisions concerning Clint's care. Clint was still capable of passing pleasurable moments with Dorothy in their home, and the family decided to delay placing him in a nursing home (even though they knew it would soon be necessary). Instead, they planned ways in which Dorothy could get relief while he remained at home.

Pastor Rue asked a member of the congregation, an attorney and trust officer in a local bank, to handle the legal issues that resulted from Clint's deteriorating mental abilities. In addition, she worked with the chair of the church's lay pastoral-care team to arrange for people to relieve Dorothy so she could get out of the house on a regular basis; she also helped Dorothy begin the process of obtaining assistance from government agencies for Clint's care.

Follow-Up

With the active intervention of the pastor, members of the congregation, and the local community, the crisis of Clint's disappearance and Dorothy's exhaustion was turned around. Eight months after Clint's walk in the woods, his deterioration reached the point where he had to be admitted to an extended-care facility. That was another loss for both of the Jacobsons, but this time they had planned in advance for the change.

Observations

This crisis not only had a dramatic precipitator (Clint's disappearance) but was complicated by Dorothy's exhaustion; she could no longer handle the strain of the constant care she gave to Clint. Up to that point life with Clint had already become a series of minor and sometimes not-so-minor incidents in which Clint did something dangerous to himself or to others, but this final event pushed her to the edge and helped her recognize that change was required.

Marion Roach has stated that "Alzheimer's disease is a disease of separation" (1987, 14). As the person dissolves, family members find themselves increasingly separated from their loved one. It places tremendous burdens upon patients and family members alike. They can expect an evolution in roles, in the ways they relate to each other interpersonally, emotionally, and intellectually, and in their plans for the future. The progressive nature of Alzheimer's disease obstructs and eventually prevents the patient's active participation in family decisions and the charting of the future.

The care of a person suffering from Alzheimer's disease exacts a considerable psychological and physical toll, and there is the potential for a series of crises over the years until death comes. The crisis can be precipitated by a dramatic event like the patient wandering off, but it can also come when the family's coping methods and resources are exhausted and a minor incident occurs—an exhaustion crisis.

A CASE OF LOST JOB SECURITY

Dennis Jackson, an eighteen-year-old junior-college freshman, was carrying a course load of seventeen hours and working twenty hours a week for an employment agency. During high school he was very involved in youth activities at church, and had known the youth pastor since early adolescence. He was living with his parents. Dennis was interested in getting at least a two-year associate of arts degree and taking general courses while deciding on his future. His pastor, Michelle Rand, considered him a well-adjusted person who was mature beyond his years. Dennis was engaged and planned to be married in about two years.

Immediate Situation

Two weeks before Dennis sought the pastor's counsel, Mr. Carlton, office manager at the employment agency where Dennis worked, quit and went to another company. Mr. Carlton asked Dennis to quit also and come to work for him. Dennis was excited about this possibility at first, especially since he had begun to feel disappointed with his new office manager, who was talking about "making some personnel changes around here." Both Dennis's parents and his fiancée noticed that he was beginning to show anxiety and was expressing dislike for his new boss. At times he felt almost paranoid: his hours were being cut, he was being "put down," and he wanted to quit. Mr. Carlton had made grand promises concerning salary, travel allowance, vacation time, and future advancement; but when Dennis began getting serious about a possible change, Mr. Carlton hedged a bit on some of these promises—though "they'd certainly be considered" when Dennis went full-time with the new company. Dennis was not even sure whether the position with Mr. Carlton would be permanent. He had reservations, and feelings of uncertainty quickly mounted. He started to panic.

Dennis's crisis was stimulated by a loss of job security. He felt he was no longer valued at his present position and felt insecure when Mr. Carlton's promises grew vague. By the time he sought out Pastor Rand, Dennis was grieving over the loss of a secure and happy job situation. His coping methods appeared exhausted. He was requesting help from everyone, including his fiancée and parents, and receiving conflicting advice.

Intervention

The night Dennis called Pastor Rand he had been struggling ineffectively all evening to write a term paper. He was so paralyzed by indecision about the job that it was affecting his schoolwork. Dennis told the pastor that he had problems and asked if they could sit down and talk as soon as possible. Pastor Rand arranged to see him between school and work the next day.

When Dennis arrived in Pastor Rand's office he was clearly at wit's end. The pastor was empathetic, and allowed him to tell the whole story. Dennis was pleased with the good relationship he had with his former boss, Mr. Carlton, but Pastor Rand raised some questions about the advisability of a change: Were conditions really that bad where he was presently employed? Were not his feelings of being put down simply a reaction to his new manager's insecurity? Would he be willing to talk with the branch manager about his relationship to the company? He also asked questions about the basic economics of the job change, especially the greater traveling distance.

After Dennis told his story, Pastor Rand helped him to boil down the many facets of his problem. The pastor stated their consensual formulation: "What I hear you saying is that you feel paralyzed by what has happened at work. You've had a good working relationship with your ex-boss, but since he left you've felt less happy, more worried and concerned. You're in a dilemma, not knowing whether you should go to work for Mr. Carlton, given all the uncertainties and the greater travel distance, or stay in your present job where you feel you might not be able to work with the new supervisor."

Dennis blurted out, "What do I do now?" Pastor Rand suggested that they needed more information before he began to act. Dennis agreed to see the general manager, Mr. Warner, and share his predicament before deciding what to do. Pastor Rand also suggested that Dennis obtain more data on the new job possibility, try to nail things down with his former employer, and come back in a couple of days to review the new information.

Two days later Dennis walked into Pastor Rand's office noticeably more upset. He had talked with Mr. Warner about his relationship with the new office manager, and instead of listening and being supportive, Mr. Warner reprimanded Dennis for coming to him without first discussing the matter with his new supervisor— and accused him of being overly suspicious and looking for trouble. The office manager had evidently told Mr. Warner some things about Dennis that were untrue, and Dennis saw right away that any defensive responses on his part would have no credibility. Mr. Carlton was also of little help, and Dennis began to suspect that he was not entirely secure in his new position.

Dennis's predicament now appeared worse; he thought he had alienated his present employer beyond reconciliation, and saw Mr. Carlton's offer vanishing before his eyes. Pastor Rand felt at this point it was imperative for Dennis to list all his options, not just the two he had presented at the outset, and to weigh them in terms of his values and goals. Some of Dennis's alternatives included looking for another job; trying to get a loan so he could quit working and concentrate on his studies; apologizing profusely to his present employer and "knuckling under" to the new regime; and accepting Mr. Carlton's offer despite its many uncertainties.

Dennis's education emerged as his dominant value and goal in this situation, and he evaluated all alternatives in the light of his return to effective functioning in school. But money, and a possible future career in personnel work, were issues he could not ignore. After weighing all possible courses of action, Dennis and Pastor Rand arrived at a compromise that he agreed to try for two months. Dennis would continue in his present position and turn down his former boss's offer. This would at least eliminate the immediate pressure of decision-making. He would attempt to be considerate of his new boss (here Pastor Rand helped to pinpoint specific behaviors Dennis could improve) and to achieve a degree of acceptance of things as they were until the semester break, when he would have time to look for another job without disrupting his studies. Dennis resigned himself to staying in his present post, "making the best of a bad situation," until summer if need be.

Follow-Up

Once Dennis had embarked upon a course of action, Pastor Rand extracted from him a promise to call her weekly to share his progress. She urged that he refrain from seeking advice from so many sources; it was only confusing him. Dennis heartily agreed.

In subsequent meetings—over the telephone and in person—Pastor Rand was able to help Dennis understand the difficulty of being a boss over a part-time employee who obviously knew more about the business than he did—and was probably more intelligent as well. Sometimes Dennis just voiced his frustrations, but usually the pastor was able to help him see how some small act on his part could make him seem less threatening to his supervisor, and therefore make his life at work more tranquil.

Observations

Pastor Rand knew Dennis well enough to recognize ways in which he was probably irritating his new supervisor, and she was not afraid to point those out to him. In the vulnerability of his crisis, Dennis did not resist her observations, but actually seemed to appreciate them. A new job did not materialize at semester break, but by then Dennis was functioning well and was content to wait for the right position to open up—understanding that few jobs are free of interpersonal stress and perhaps none is ideal.

Dennis's crisis was not resolved through any significant external change in his environment or circumstances; what did change was Dennis's perception of the situation and his active utilization of coping methods designed to keep his life on an even keel so he could concentrate on what he valued most.

A CASE OF ATTEMPTED SUICIDE

Pastor Kurt Anderson was exhausted from all the activities of a usual Sunday—two services, a special church council meeting in the afternoon, and the youth group that evening. It was close to midnight when he went to bed. Within minutes, just as he began to slide into that delightful phase halfway between wakefulness and sleep, the telephone rang. The caller was Rick Patton, age forty-seven, phoning about his forty-five-year-old wife, Rebecca. They had been married over twenty years and had no children. Pastor Anderson had never met or talked with the couple before.

Immediate Situation

The speech at the other end of the line was excited and rapid. Rick blurted, "My wife has taken a lot of pills—I don't know what to do." The crisis precipitator for Rick was the threatened (and potentially real) loss of the most significant relationship in his life. He perceived the potential loss as disastrous. His coping methods were temporarily paralyzed. He had done nothing for the first five minutes; then he thought of calling Pastor Anderson, whose name had been given to him four weeks before when the couple moved from Wisconsin to Florida.

Intervention

Before Pastor Anderson was able to intervene, he had to deal with his own apprehensive feelings. The adrenaline flowed through his body, and he found himself asking mainly informational questions of Rick. For the first minute or two the pastor too was paralyzed; he had read what to do in a suicide situation and he had counseled several people who had threatened suicide, but this was his first experience with someone who had actually done something destructive to herself. Just as Pastor Anderson's anxiety eased a bit and he felt better able to cope with the situation, the caller thrust the phone into his wife's hand. So far Pastor Anderson had learned who the caller was (name and address) and what he was calling about. He had asked what the drug was (Secanol), how many were taken (remainder of bottle, number unknown), and when (five or ten minutes previously).

But when Rebecca Patton took the phone she was able only to mumble incoherently. Pastor Anderson could not understand what she was saying. He tried yelling into the phone to arouse her. Then he heard a thud and the clunk of the receiver as it hit the floor. Evidently she had collapsed into unconsciousness.

Kurt Anderson had been on the phone now for four or five minutes. He had little time to develop a relationship. He realized that he had to take a directive role. When Rick came back to the phone screaming that his wife had passed out, Kurt said, "OK. Here is what we are going to do." The pastor could not wait for Rick to mobilize his coping abilities; he gently but firmly gave orders.

Pastor Anderson first told Rick to make sure that his wife's breathing passage was not blocked and that she was still breathing. Then he told him to leave their phone connection open, go to a neighbor's house, tell the neighbor what had happened, and enlist help. Rick balked at this suggestion, saying he had only been in town a short time and did not know his neighbors. Pastor Anderson responded, "Listen, your wife's life is in danger—don't worry about things like that. People are usually willing to help in a time of crisis." Pastor Anderson called 911 on his cell phone while Rick was at the neighbors.

After two or three minutes that seemed like an eternity, Rick returned to the phone. He had enlisted the help of a married couple who lived next door; a police car was already pulling up in front, and Rick had to hang up. Pastor Anderson requested that Rick call him from the hospital.

At 1:30 A.M. Pastor Anderson's phone rang again. Rick said the ambulance had arrived very quickly, his wife's stomach was pumped, and the doctor said she was going to be all right but had to stay overnight at the hospital. Pastor Anderson suggested that she needed to see a counselor immediately upon discharge from the hospital. Rick said she had already made an appointment to see a psychologist, but that appointment was still two weeks away. Pastor Anderson let him know that most psychotherapists will see a person sooner if a crisis exists, and he strongly recommended that Rick call the psychologist first thing in the morning. Rick agreed to do so.

Follow-Up

Early Monday afternoon Pastor Anderson called Rick. He learned that Rebecca was already out of the hospital and was seeing the psychologist that very afternoon. Pastor Anderson told Rick to call him if he could be of any further help. Later that week, he stopped by their home to invite them to church and see about other ways he could assist them with their move to town.

Observations

It is obvious from this case that active intervention was absolutely necessary. The pastor temporarily took responsibility for and control of the situation—he gave orders. Fortunately Rick trusted the pastor enough to follow these orders—a good example of the lowered level of defensiveness and heightened psychological accessibility a person experiences during a crisis (chapter 2). Few people would be so trusting of a stranger in ordinary circumstances.

Kurt's questions to Rick about the attempted suicide were specific: "With what?" "How much?" "How long ago?" Getting exact information and precise details are always important in a suicidal crisis so that an appropriate intervention can be shaped from the information (chapter 4). Finally, the pastor called 911 rather than an ambulance because he knew that in their city, as in many cities, the 911 dispatcher automatically notifies the fire department, the police, and an ambulance in a suicide attempt. As a result, three sources of help were soon rushing to the scene.

A CASE OF A CHILD'S REACTION TO A MOVE

Pastor Sally Carpenter was an assistant minister at a large downtown church in a midwestern city. She was responsible for Christian education and also served as counselor for the church's parochial school.

On many mornings Pastor Carpenter would walk through the halls of the school, greeting and being greeted by the children as they arrived. One Monday morning Patty, a six-year-old in the first grade, greeted Pastor Carpenter as usual and then added, "I have some bad news to tell you." When Pastor Carpenter asked what it was, Patty said: "My father has left home for a while." The pastor asked why, and Patty replied: "Because he has to work out of town."

Pastor Carpenter did not know Patty's parents well. Patty had two brothers attending the school—Matthew, eight, and Peter, eleven. She was shy but always greeted Pastor Carpenter with a smile. Patty did not seem very upset that morning, and the pastor continued walking down the hall greeting other children.

Immediate Situation

The next day, Patty's teacher came to Pastor Carpenter's office and related the following series of incidents. On the day before, Patty also had told him that her father had "gone away for a while." He did not pursue it because it did not seem to bother her, but that morning Patty asked the school secretary to call him out of the lounge before school started. Patty told her teacher that her father had come back home but "he doesn't love me anymore." When the teacher asked why she said that, Patty replied that her father had beaten her with his hand. The teacher brought her to the school nurse, who could find no signs of a beating. Throughout that morning Patty told the teacher one story after another, each more fantastic than the last: "The house burned down," "My mother almost died last night." Whenever the teacher discredited a story, Patty simply said she was kidding and laughed.

This behavior was atypical for Patty, who was generally rather withdrawn. Finally, just before lunch, Patty began to cry and said her stomach hurt and she felt sick. When the teacher asked if she wanted to go home, she screamed that she had no home and hated everybody, especially her father. The teacher brought Patty to the nurse's office and sought the assistance of Pastor Carpenter.

Intervention

After Pastor Carpenter and the teacher talked for a few minutes, they went down to the nurse's office to meet Patty. Pastor Carpenter related to Patty that her teacher had told her all the fantastic tales she had been telling, and asked, "Is something bothering you?" Responding to the pastor's skill in empathetically talking with children, Patty finally opened up. During the past weekend, her family had moved from their apartment to a house. For the parents it was an exciting move because they were finally in their own home. It appeared, however, that no one in the family had taken the time to tell Patty anything about the move or why it was necessary. The loss of a familiar environment and of her friends in the apartment building was difficult for Patty to cope with. Her sense of security was threatened. She viewed her father as the culprit, because he was the one who physically moved her things.

Patty was very close to her brother Matt, and the teacher suggested that Matt come to their class that afternoon. Her other brother, Peter, joined them as well. The brothers shared information about the move with Patty and the other children. The teacher also read stories about moving, and the entire class shared in Patty's experience. Patty discovered that two children in her class now lived a few houses away from her.

Meanwhile, Pastor Carpenter called the mother, explained the situation, and offered to stop by, but the mother was too embarrassed about their messy house to have a visitor. Pastor Carpenter suggested that the family, especially the father, talk with Patty about the move. The mother was responsive to the call and said they would talk that evening.

Follow-Up

Pastor Carpenter was prepared to recommend family therapy for Patty if her problems continued, but when she checked back with Patty's teacher during the next few days he indicated that Patty was back to her old self. Patty's parents never called the pastor back, but at the parent-teacher conference three weeks later the teacher learned that they had talked at length that Tuesday evening at the supper table, and Patty did not seem to have any further problem.

Observations

Reviewing the case in the light of the A-B-C method, one can see that Pastor Carpenter had already apparently achieved a relationship with Patty, although no more than a few words each day had passed between them. The pastor had a natural ability for relating with children. Once she knew the facts, she boiled down Patty's problem: "You feel bad because you don't have your same house or your same friends anymore," and "You are mad at your daddy for making the move." To the latter statement Patty had blurted out her definite response to the formulation: "Yeah!"

The pastor and the teacher mutually took responsibility for forming a method of action. They set up situations where Patty could not only talk about her loss but also received the support of others. Because crises happen not only to individuals but also to families, they arranged for Patty to have a chance to talk about what was happening with her brothers first and then with her parents later the same day.

The teacher was very cooperative and empathetic in handling Patty. After becoming aware of Patty's problem, the parents were apparently also responsive to her feelings. The resolution of the crisis was worked out in a matter of hours, and Patty was back to her usual self thereafter.

A CASE OF A TORNADO IN A SMALL TOWN

Residents of north central Texas know what it's like to live in "tornado alley." At certain times of the year, we know that a tornado can form at almost any time. Perhaps it's no different from living with the threat of earthquakes in California or hurricanes along the Gulf Coast. When a tornado hits a large metropolitan area like the Dallas/Fort Worth Metroplex or Oklahoma City, it tends to strike a discrete section of the city, allowing emergency services from all over the city and county to respond. No matter how devastating the damage, it usually does not stop aid from coming. But when a "monster tornado" hits a small town, the impact is total. Frequently, those who are called upon to respond to the crisis (such as pastoral caregivers) are to a greater or lesser extent victims of the crisis themselves.

Immediate Situation

Warning sirens went off at 1:40 one Wednesday afternoon in a North Texas town of less than five thousand people. Fifteen minutes later a huge tornado tore through the center of town, destroying the majority of homes and businesses there and damaging many of those that were left standing. It flattened City Hall (which housed the communication and emergency services) as well as the Baptist church and other buildings, and partially destroyed the Disciples of Christ church. Fortunately the school was at the edge of town and was for the most part spared. Everybody lost electricity and telephone services for days.

Intervention

Although the crisis wrought by this "monster tornado" called for many responders in and outside of the community, this case will focus on the Disciples of Christ minister, Roger Gordon, and the pastoral care he offered.

When the siren sounded, Roger was at home working on his sermon and answering emails. He did not react to the siren immediately, but when he looked out and saw the dark green-gray sky, he became concerned. His wife Anette checked the radar on the local weather channel and yelled that they should go to the interior bathroom that they had pre-determined was the safest place in the house. They took shelter there and waited out the deafening storm. Those few minutes were an eternity.

When the Gordons emerged from their bathroom after the tornado had passed, they looked up at the sky. A big chunk of their roof was gone, and heavy rain was dousing their possessions. But Roger and Anette were among the more fortunate citizens of their town. Stepping outside, they heard cries from the house across the street and realized that their 89-year-old neighbor was buried under the rubble that had been his bedroom. They tried to telephone for help, but neither their home phone nor their cell phones would work. So the Gordons and a couple of other neighbors went to work. They removed bricks and timbers from the direction of the cries and were able to free the trapped man. He had suffered many bruises and, they later learned, a broken arm and several broken ribs. While Mrs. Gordon and a friend stayed with the injured man and tried to make him comfortable, Pastor Gordon walked the four blocks to the church to see if he could make a phone call there (the roads were impassable, covered with trees and debris, and a tree rested on their SUV). Along the half-mile walk he observed or participated in several other rescues of people and animals caught in flattened homes.

Arriving at the church, Roger discovered considerable damage. One entire wall had collapsed. Later, Roger learned that the collapsed wall had trapped and killed a passerby who had sought refuge there.

Follow-Up

Four people were killed in the tornado, and many more were injured. The first task of pastoral caregiving was to get medical care for trapped and injured people. All normal communication systems were down, but an amateur radio operator who was a member of Roger's congregation and lived nearby was able to make contact with the outside world from the radio transceiver in his car. Over the next few weeks, Pastor Gordon spent virtually all of his time visiting members of the congregation and townsfolk, listening to their stories. There were also hospital calls on the injured, visits with the bereaved, and funerals for those who had died. As the weeks passed, Roger's listening ministry led to advocacy with insurance and governmental organizations for those whose property was damaged, and counseling with those who had lost their homes and faced important decisions, such as the choice to rebuild or move away from Tornado Alley.

Observations

What do you do when crisis happens to you as well as others? Pastor Gordon described walking through the town after the tornado and embracing neighbors and members of the congregation, tears flowing until he was too exhausted to cry. For months afterward he worked from morning to night in this small Texas town, caring for others until "I had nothing left." He was exhausted. He (and often his wife) had cared for everyone else but had not been cared for. He was busy all the time and yet could never do enough. People were wonderful and loving, but he could not relax enough to let anyone —not even his own family—care for him.

Pastor Gordon carried on for about a year after the tornado. Then, burned out, he resigned from the church and took a leave of absence from ministry. He sought counseling and took a breather.

Such burnout is a built-in danger for caregivers in times of crisis, especially following natural disasters, school shootings, terrorist attacks, or devastating accidents such as bus or airline crashes that impact a large number of people in a community. Sooner or later, caregiver overload will afflict pastors who take seriously their ministry of care to those in crisis but neglect their own needs, fail to take time off, refuse to allow others to care for them. Large-scale tragedies are hard on all responders—as our nation learned from the 9/11 terrorist attack in New York City—but doubly so when the helpers are involved in the crisis as Pastor Gordon and his family were. Pastor Gordon is a skilled and compassionate pastoral caregiver, but he still needed the pastoral care of others. Long after his car was replaced, his house repaired, and the church building rebuilt, Roger's spirit was in need of repair and replenishment. Years have gone by since then; Pastor Gordon has returned to ministry but as a wiser pastor who ensures that he is cared for even as he tends the needs of others. He no longer lives in Tornado Alley.

These cases of people in crisis represent a wide range of ages, backgrounds, resources, and situations. But they share more than a casual observer might detect—a sense of loss or threatened loss, for example. All responded well to some variation of the crisis-management strategies presented herein; all returned to their pre-crisis stability. In the process of resolving their crises, most did more than get back to the way they were; they also experienced emotional and spiritual growth, and increased strength to face future challenges.

6

THE CHURCH
AS CARING COMMUNITY

Let us give thanks to the God and Father of our Lord Jesus
Christ, the merciful Father, the God from whom all help
comes! He helps us in all our troubles, so that we are able
to help others who have all kinds of troubles, using the
same help that we ourselves have received from God.

—2 Cor. 1:3-4, TEV

Because God's love for us is a prior condition for our loving others, the congregation is an instrument through which God's love is
translated to those in need. In many ways the church, as a caring
community, is singularly well suited for responding to people in
crisis.

A STUDY OF CHURCH MEMBERS
DURING TIMES OF CRISIS

Recently, I joined forces with two psychology professors and one
communications professor at Texas Christian University to investi-
gate how the church responds to people in crisis (Stone et al. 2003;
Stone et al. 2004). The purpose of the research was to understand
what church members experience during a situational crisis and
to identify the resources of social support that are helpful for them
during times of crisis. We examined traditional sources of help as
well as resources associated with religion. The study served as a
test of the theory discussed in this book.

By identifying the degree to which personal religious beliefs
and participation in a particular congregation help people in crisis, this study sought to provide a foundation from which religious
as well as mental health professionals can understand the psychological benefits of religious involvement. Certainly the church
already understands that spiritual benefits accrue from regular
involvement in religious activities; this study focused especially
on the psychological benefits of belief and involvement in a faith

community for those experiencing a life crisis. Specifically, we sought to identify factors, both religious and secular, that help to mitigate the stress and risk associated with acute life crises.

The study was carried out from September 1999 to May 2000. All twenty-six participants in the study belonged to a suburban, seven hundred-member Southern Baptist congregation. All had experienced the onset of a crisis event within the previous two weeks at the time of the first interview. Later, after the crisis had passed, they received a follow-up interview.

The church members interviewed for the study reported what helped and supported them in coping with their crises. Certainly there were differences from one individual to another; however, the following key themes appeared in at least half of the participants' responses. Some will be obvious to readers and others may be surprising (they were to us!).

The Presence of Others

The presence of others was one of the two or three most beneficial resources that helped church members get through their crisis. Most people in the study gained emotional support and anchoring in their faith through the friendship and acts of kindness offered by friends, family members, and small groups. For some of the participants, the presence and involvement of family and friends provided the most important social support. For others, members of their congregation provided the greatest support. Almost all of the participants reported some of both.

Social support from the involvement of others took many forms. One friend sat with the person in the ICU waiting room; another cleaned house for the family; many brought or prepared food; still others showed their support by just being with the one in crisis.

In this particular congregation, every active member belongs to a shepherd group, a small "family" of twenty to thirty people with a trained leader that meets once a month to share food, fellowship, Bible study, prayer, and hymn singing; they also tend one another when a member is in difficulty. On a number of crisis occasions, members of a shepherd group arrived at the hospital or home before the subject's family members. In one case a woman called to tell the shepherd group leader what was happening before she left for the hospital. These groups are a way for people living in a fragmented, urban society to feel anchored to a small but significant community; they also are a way to personalize the church (especially where the congregation is large).

Prayer

Prayer was one of the most universally helpful sources of strength and support for the church members in the study. Three types of prayer experience sustained them. First, participants found the *act of praying* to be important. The primary purpose of their prayers was to experience the presence of God; they also prayed for a sense of peace as well as confidence that they would be able to handle the situation.

Second, the subjects valued the knowledge that *others were praying for them.* Members of the congregation who called or visited them would say, "I'm praying for you." In this particular congregation the Prayer Circle (an organization of praying groups within the church) mobilizes whenever a crisis occurs, and persons in crisis know that a number of church members are praying for them by name. Most participants indicated that this knowledge was very comforting.

In the third type of prayer experience *a minister, pastoral caregiver, or fellow church member prayed with them.* Even though ministers prayed with all of the participants, most of them referred especially to laypersons who came and prayed with them in the hospital, at the funeral home, in their homes, at work, and so on. People came to be with them and offer physical assistance, to be sure, but they also offered to pray with them and thus nourished and supported them spiritually.

In short, prayer was one of the most important sources of support for the church members of this study. The second and third types of prayer experience—knowing that others were praying for them and having someone actually pray with them—appeared to be most important. When everything was falling apart and these people could not figure out how to (or if they could) handle a situation, they were able to pray. It may be significant that the participants belonged to a church that prays regularly, and were themselves in the habit of prayer. The skill of prayer had been developed over many years and appeared to provide significant support and anchoring in their times of crisis.

An important component of the participants' prayer life was their view of God. When people in the study talked about God, they almost seemed to be talking about two distinct Gods. First, they wanted to have a sense of an *immanent* God who would be present with them in this difficult time. Many of them referred to Jesus as the one who, because of his own suffering, could understand their pain. These individuals wanted to experience a personal relationship with a God who would be with them very personally during their crisis.

They also spoke of a *transcendent* God, one who is in control. "Only God knows why this is happening to me," one respondent said. In fact, most of the participants appeared to want a personal *and* a powerful God, with them in their troubles but also in charge and able to change the situation. One woman described her faith in this way: "I knew I wasn't going to get through the day without God. . . . I lived dependent on, I couldn't breathe without God. . . . there was no fathomable other way to deal with that kind of pain." That some might consider a close, immanent God and a more distant, powerful God to be somewhat of a contradiction theologically did not seem to bother these people, at least not in their crises.

Acts of Kindness

The authors were struck by the many and varied acts of kindness offered by family, friends, and members of the congregation (bringing a cake or hot dish, driving a child to flute lesson, cleaning up the kitchen or the house, taking care of children while the parent or parents dealt with the crisis). At first it appeared that these acts of kindness simply took a burden off those in crisis so they could focus on their more pressing needs. Soon, however, we became aware that they were perceived as *acts of solidarity or support*—a physical way of expressing concern, love, and care.

Just as knowing that others are praying for you is crucial not only for the act of prayer but because it communicates that others are concerned for your well-being, an act of kindness like preparing a meal, babysitting, or doing yard work goes beyond simple help or nourishment to communicate how much the giver cares.

The authors of the study reflected that ministers who exhort their congregations to love neighbor and put faith into action often omit an important hermeneutic task: to bless people for the many ways in which they *already act in love*. Many people sitting in the pews are quietly acting out their faith in varied and profound ways, often more than they are given credit for. Many of them do not understand that these simple, physical acts of caring are the very essence of loving neighbor, of a ministry of presence, which their pastors often exhort them to perform (Stone 1996).

Music

The first few times we read over the transcripts, the study's authors overlooked the impact of music on those in crisis. After several subsequent readings, however, we noticed that about half of the subjects described how music sustained them during their troubles. Some reflected on the words and images of a hymn. Others turned on a tape and listened to Christian music. One woman described being in the intensive-care unit, filled with fear that she was going to die. She was unable to sleep even with the help of sleep medications. Only when her family played some of her favorite tapes of Christian music could she relax and finally sleep at night.

Hymns and other Christian music are poetic ways of communicating key themes of the faith. When beliefs were shaken by the horror of a crisis, familiar hymns helped participants hold on to their faith. Frequently, it was the thoughts contained in the music that were most important. Hymns help people anchor the meaning of the faith. Music allows them to process experiences, beliefs, and reflections faster and at a deeper level.

Resilience

Sometimes, in our psychologically oriented culture, it is easy to believe that psychopathology hides under every rock of human experience and people will fall apart when facing a difficult time. That certainly was not true with the individuals in this study. In fact, they showed great resilience. All but one made it through the crisis without seeking professional psychotherapy. Indeed, these people mustered considerable strength and capability to address their crises. They met their crises head-on. A number of participants possessed confidence that they could get through this crisis, and most people realized that they had made it through past crises. And they placed their confidence in a suffering God who is with them in their pain and suffering.

Empathy

A number of participants also recognized that some of their helpers—members of the church or family members—had come through similar crises. They drew strength from the helper and recognized that their own crisis could be similarly weathered. One very young couple found that many of their friends, who had never known loss or hard times, seemed to be somewhat frightened off by their very difficult situation and drifted away from them during the crisis. Older members of a Sunday school group, all of whom had experienced multiple crises in their lives, responded to this young husband and wife, invited them to social events, and cared for them and provided the support that they were not able to get from their same-age friends. The empathy and compassion of pastoral caregivers, family, and friends was critical for many of the church members when they experienced a crisis.

THE CHURCH'S MINISTRY

Thomas F. McGee (Caplan 1964, 151), a mental health professional specializing in crisis work, describes four conditions essential for effective crisis intervention. The first is *location*. For crisis intervention to be effective, persons doing it must be involved with and located in a specific community; people in crisis—probably because of their paralysis, immobility, and difficulties in problem solving—rely upon helpers or agencies that are readily accessible.

Second is *availability*. Individuals in crisis must be able quickly to achieve contact with those who can help—during the period of crisis, not two or three weeks later; these moments of heightened psychological accessibility require less care or counseling effort than after the crisis triangle has tipped back to its base (see diagram 3 on p. 19).

A third condition is *mobility*. The counselor who sits in a mental health center waiting for people in crisis to show up is not able to take part in comprehensive crisis intervention. Those who help in crises must be able to go to the scene of a crisis, roll up their sleeves, and do what is needed—even to recognize and intervene in a crisis when no help has been requested.

Fourth, *flexibility of procedure* is needed. Crisis intervention requires a variety of means and methods, such as walk-in clinics, telephone calls, home visits, fifteen-minute supportive sessions, and use of paraprofessionals—as many resources and support systems as possible.

Frequently, trained clergy and laypersons within congregations can meet McGee's four conditions for effective crisis intervention more effectively than can helpers in the traditional mental health community. One of the chief advantages of the church in crisis intervention is its location. For centuries, it been known as the place where people in distress can go for sanctuary, hospitality, and assistance.

Associated with the church is not only its pastor but also a whole system of concerned people who can be mobilized in a short period of time to care for others. From the standpoint of crisis intervention, this availability is a benefit because people in crisis generally can see the minister or a lay pastoral caregiver within a day or two, if not immediately.

The church as a community of saints has always been a movable institution. Ministers and laypersons can go to the scene of a crisis, whether it is an accident or disaster, a hospital room, a school, or the workplace. In fact, they are expected to be present at the time of a death. In one case of the study described above, members from the church arrived at the hospital before family members showed up. The church's ministry is not closed up in the sanctuary; it branches out into the whole community. From the beginning, Christian fellowship has occurred "where two or three are gathered in my name" (Matt. 18:20).

Mental health professionals are now beginning to realize the necessity of flexibility in procedure; at one time many therapists who thought they were very flexible and eclectic counselors did most of their counseling within the four walls of an office for fifty-minute sessions of face-to-face contact. They rarely took advantage of intervention methods that the church has historically used, such as home and hospital visits, letter writing or telephone calls, visitation by laypersons (paraprofessionals), and incorporation of the needy person into a group of caring individuals.

The purpose of the church is to increase and promote among all people the love of God and each other. The church helps to communicate this love in real and concrete ways to individuals in crisis so that they can respond in turn with increased love for

God and others. The three traditional tasks of the church have been defined as *kerygma* (teaching and proclaiming the gospel), *koinonia* (fellowship), and *diakonia* (implementing the faith in Christian love and service). Crisis intervention realizes all three forms of ministry. It proceeds primarily out of love and service (*diakonia*), but it also helps individuals relate better with others as a part of the community of God (*koinonia*), and it facilitates new learning (*kerygma*) at a time when people are especially open to hearing the word. It is within the local church fellowship, and not only through the minister, that persons can come to know and care for one another in a way that makes genuine Christian community possible and stretches the pastoral-care ministry beyond what the pastor does alone.

THE MINISTRY OF THE LAITY

The crisis caregiver does not have to be an ordained minister or a mental health professional. Laypersons doing crisis work are a natural extension of the church's network of care. Crisis centers and suicide prevention agencies have discovered the value of using volunteers from many walks of life—housewives, attorneys, construction workers, businesspeople—who are trained specifically in crisis intervention methods. The pastor who would extend the caring ministry of the local parish beyond what one person can accomplish can enlist and train many others to help in times of crisis.

One of the most beneficial ways of empowering members of the congregation in crisis intervention work is to gather a small cluster of lay pastoral carers and train them in intervention methods. Space here does not permit a detailed description of such a training program for lay pastoral care ministry; I have covered that subject in another book (Stone 1991). Such a training program should involve not only didactic input but also the use of role play, as well as teaching and practicing the A-B-C method of crisis intervention counseling. In this regard, the pastor can present typical cases (see chapter 5) for discussion in class. Telephone intervention role-play can be practiced by seating the participants back-to-back, thus preventing them from relying on facial or other visual, nonverbal clues.

Crisis lay pastoral carers can respond to the distinct needs of individual congregations, for example, by calling on the sick and shut-in, being with people after a death in a family, and visiting an extended-care facility. Crisis lay caregivers can also be trained in general pastoral care visitation; they can develop and use their skills for helping shut-ins and others who are lonely but not experiencing a crisis.

Lay pastoral carers need to have ongoing supervision and feedback. Supervision occurs best in a group setting—except in emergencies, when ministers can consult by phone or in person. Actually, crisis intervention training never ceases; but after the initial training sessions the training transitions from weekly classes to monthly supervision and ad hoc consultation. In discussing the training of paraprofessionals for crisis intervention, Edwin Shneidman (1973, 11) writes, "What you need is a good heart, freedom from proselytizing for your own private causes, supervised training focused on crisis intervention, and a pinch of wisdom. . . . Three pre-conditions are essential: careful selection, rigorous training, and continuous ruthless supervision."

If laypersons are to function successfully as crisis interveners in congregations, their ministers must not feel threatened by working with laypersons who are competent to do some pastoral care tasks. They must convey to their parishioners that ministry is a function of the whole people of God, the priesthood of all believers. Every Christian is commissioned to care for others. The lay pastoral care ministry does not necessarily cut down on the amount of pastoral care visitation required of ministers—it may well increase it—but can ultimately offer the congregation a broader-based, more inclusive pastoral care ministry.

The pastor and congregation can be involved in crisis work in a variety of other ways. For example, members of the congregation can serve on the board of a mental health center. They can help encourage local crisis or mental health centers to be more effective and relevant to the community, offering help to all people and not just the privileged or the insured. Churchpeople can establish and serve on hotlines or crisis intervention centers in communities where none presently exist. They can serve on existing crisis hotlines or other programs that need volunteer help within the community. They can develop prayer groups that respond to the congregation's as well as the community's needs.

The group effort of a caring congregation for those in crisis can become an example of convergence behavior, a phenomenon that frequently occurs after natural disasters (like Hurricane Katrina), in which there is an influx of people who are eager to help, are looking for friends and relatives, or are simply curious. Convergence behavior rarely occurs spontaneously in cases of emotional crisis, but in a congregation it can be fostered. Helpers engage anyone they can to meet the troubled persons' needs and to reassure them that they have not been abandoned.

Such deep and genuine fellowship is an expression of *koinonia*. In the New Testament Paul speaks of the participation and mutual fellowship among believers, stemming from the relationship of each believer with Christ. *Koinonia* is possible today among people who come together from all walks of life to share in one central concern. It is especially important in times of crisis, when a troubled person needs a sense of belonging and fellowship with other Christians.

One dimension of *koinonia* is partnership. All Christians are partners in Christ. Even in the pastoral care relationship, the helper and the helped alike give to and receive from each other. *Koinonia* is always active, never passive or stagnant. It is spontaneous and uncontrived; it is not inward but exists in relationships where sharing and reaching out occur; it is vigorous and honest and can involve—even require—encounters between people.

The potential for *koinonia* exists within all people. Out of it trust develops. As a result of it, people can go to each other for succor in crises. Wherever *koinonia* exists within a Christian community, pastoral care naturally becomes a function of the entire congregation; people reach out to each other in their crises as well as in their day-to-day troubles, despair, hope, and joy.

Crisis intervention, whether undertaken by members of the congregation, the clergy, or both, is a core task of ministry aimed at encountering and caring for the many people in each community who experience crises. It is an important way in which Christians can express the love of God to persons at their times of greatest need.

BIBLIOGRAPHY

Aden, L. (1968). "Pastoral Counseling as Christian Perspective." In Homans 1968, 163–81.

Bonhoeffer, D. (1978). *Life Together.* San Francisco: Harper & Row.

Caplan, G. (1964). *Principles of Preventive Psychiatry.* New York: Basic. The second chapter, "A Conceptual Model for Primary Prevention," describes the characteristics of significant life crises and factors that influence their outcome.

Caplan, G., E. Mason, and D. Kaplan (1965). "Four Studies of Crisis in Parents of Prematures." *Community Mental Health Journal* 1, no. 2 (Summer): 149–61.

Clinebell, H. (1966 & 1984). *Basic Types of Pastoral Care and Counseling.* Nashville: Abingdon. Chapter 8 suggests several different approaches to crisis counseling.
N.d. *New Approaches to Crisis Counseling* (film). Pastoral Care in Crisis Film Series. Columbus: Community Mental Health Services, distributors.

Everstine, D., and L. Everstine (2006). *Strategic Interventions for People in Crisis, Trauma, and Disaster.* Rev. ed. New York: Routledge.

Farberow, N., S. Heilig, and R. Litman (1968). *Techniques in Crisis Intervention: A Training Manual.* Los Angeles: Suicide Prevention Center, Inc.

Frankl, V. (1997). *Man's Search for Meaning.* New York: Washington Square.

Gerkin, C. (1987). *Crisis Experience in Modern Life: Theory and Theology for Pastoral Care.* Nashville: Abingdon. An excellent book on a theological understanding of life crises.

Gilliand, B., and R. James (2004). *Crisis Intervention Strategies:* 5th ed. Belmont: Wadsworth. One of the best books on crisis.

Halpern, H. (1973). "Crisis Theory: A Definitional Study." *Community Mental Health Journal* 9, no. 4 (Winter): 342–49.

Hoff, L. A. (2001). *People in Crisis: Clinical and Public Health Perspectives.* San Francisco: Jossey-Bass.

Homans, P., ed. (1968). *The Dialogue Between Theology and Psychology*. Chicago: University of Chicago Press.

Jacobson, G. (1965). "Crisis Theory and Treatment Strategy: Some Socio-Cultural and Psychodynamic Considerations." *The Journal of Nervous and Mental Diseases* 141, no.2: 214–15.

Jeter, J. R. (1998). *Crisis Preaching: Personal and Public*. Nashville: Abingdon.

Jones, W. (1968). "The A-B-C Method of Crisis Management." *Mental Hygiene* 52 (January): 87–89.

Jung, C. (1949). *Modern Man in Search of a Soul*. London: Routledge & Kegan Paul.

Kalicki, A., ed. (1987). *Confronting Alzheimer's Disease*. Owings Mills, Md.: National Health Publishing.

Lazarus, R. (1966). *Psychological Stress and the Coping Process*. New York: McGraw-Hill. A ponderous but valuable volume that details a cognitive theorist's view of stress; discusses primary and secondary appraisal of perceived threat.

Lester, D., ed. (2002). *Crisis Intervention and Counseling by Telephone*. 2d ed. Springfield: Charles C. Thomas.

Morley, W. E. (1970). "Theory of Crisis Intervention." *Pastoral Psychology* 21, no. 203: 16.

O'Hanlon, W. and M. Weiner-Davis (2003). *In Search of Solutions*. 2d ed. New York: Norton. Although not a book on crisis intervention per se, it provides a good introduction to brief counseling.

Parad, H., ed. (1965). *Crisis Intervention: Selected Readings*. New York: Family Service Association of America.

Parad, H., and L. Parad, eds. (2005). *Crisis Intervention Book 2: The Practitioner's Sourcebook for Brief Therapy*. Tucson: Fenestra.

Pastoral Psychology 21. April 1970. The entire issue of this journal is devoted to the minister and crisis intervention; included are articles by Gerald Jacobson ("Crisis Intervention from the Viewpoint of the Mental Health Professional"), Wilbur Morley ("Theory of Crisis Intervention"), and David K. Switzer ("Crisis Intervention Techniques for the Minister").

Pittman, F. (1987). *Turning Points: Treating Families in Transition and Crisis*. New York: Norton. Provides a systems approach to handling crises that considers the impact of a particular crisis on the family as a whole.

Roach, M. (1987). "Another Name for Madness." In Kalicki 1987, xv–xxi.

Roberts, A., ed. (2005). *Crisis Intervention Handbook: Assessment, Treatment and Research*. Oxford: Oxford University Press. Includes a wide variety of information on crisis prepared by a team of fifty well-respected crisis and trauma experts.

Rusk, T. (1971). "Opportunity and Technique in Crisis Psychiatry." *Comprehensive Psychiatry* 12 (May): 249–63.

Shneidman, E. (1973). "Crisis Intervention: Some Thoughts and Perspectives." In Specter and Claiborn 1973.

Specter, G., and W. Claiborn, eds. (1973). *Crisis Intervention*. New York: Behavioral Publications.

Stone, H. W. (1972). *Suicide and Grief*. Philadelphia: Fortress.

———— (1991). *The Caring Church: A Guide for Lay Pastoral Care*. Minneapolis: Fortress Press. The book describes a program of training laypersons in pastoral care.

———— (1994). *Brief Pastoral Counseling*. Minneapolis: Fortress Press. This book and Stone 2001 present a way to offer brief care and counseling for people who are not in crisis. It is a companion to this book, *Crisis Counseling*.

———— (1996). *The Theological Context of Pastoral Care*. New York: Haworth. The book presents a theological understanding of pastoral care ministry.

———— (2001). *Strategies for Brief Pastoral Counseling*. Minneapolis: Fortress Press.

Stone, H. W., D. Cross, K. Purvis, and M. Young (2003). "A Study of the Benefits of Social and Religious Support on Church Members During Times of Crisis." *Pastoral Psychology* 51, no. 4: 327–40. This research study and the one following describe the impact that crises have upon individuals and families in a mainline protestant church in Texas. What clergy and church members did that was helpful is detailed.

———— (2004). "A Study of Church Members During Times of Crisis." *Pastoral Psychology*, 52, no. 5: 405–21.

Stone, H. W. and J. Duke (2006). *How to Think Theologically*. 2d ed. Minneapolis: Fortress Press. A basic text on how to do theological reflection. Easy to understand.

Switzer, D. (1986). *The Minister as Crisis Counselor*. New York: Abingdon. An excellent volume covering all aspects of a intervention in the crises of parishioners.

⸻ (2000). *Pastoral Care Emergencies*. Creative Pastoral Care and Counseling. Minneapolis: Fortress Press.

LaVergne, TN USA
14 June 2010
185877LV00011B/1/P